Beth's Basic Bread Book

Beth's Basic Bread Book

Simple Techniques and Simply Delicious Recipes for Foolproof Baking

BETH HENSPERGER

PHOTOGRAPHY BY ILISA KATZ

ILLUSTRATIONS BY GEORGIA DEAVER

CHRONICLE BOOKS
SAN FRANCISCO

Ilisa Katz wishes to extend her special thanks to Mariann Sauvion and Lisa Silvestri for bringing their exceptional baking and styling talents to this book, to Catherine Hayn for her superb assistance, to Wolfman Gold for the use of its beautiful wares, and to Steve Rissman and Barbara Katz for their continued love and support.

Printed in Hong Kong.

Library of Congress Cataloging-in-Publication Data:
Hensperger, Beth.
      Beth's basic bread book: simple techniques and simply delicious recipes for foolproof baking/Beth Hensperger;
      photography by Ilisa Katz; illustrations by Georgia Deaver.
              p. cm.
      Includes index.
      ISBN 0-8118-0820-3 (pbk.)
      1. Bread. I. title.
TX769.H435 1996
641.8'15-dc20   95-47744
                                          CIP

Design: Gretchen Scoble
Composition: On Line Type

Distributed in Canada by Raincoast Books, 8680 Cambie St., Vancouver, B.C. V6P 6M9

10 9 8 7 6 5 4 3 2 1

Chronicle Books
275 Fifth Street
San Francisco, CA 94103

I would like to dedicate this work to the memory of my father

EDWARD S. HENSPERGER

1925–1994

❈

Acknowledgments

❁

Many thanks goes to the great teamwork of Bill LeBlond and Leslie Jonath, who combine a working relationship with lots of patience and skill; and to Susan Derecskey for her meticulous copy editing.

I wish to pay special tribute to the encouragement, kindness, and unwavering vision of Martha Casselman, an outstanding literary agent and true friend.

Special thanks to the experienced bread testing/tasting provided by Judy Adam, Katherine Petersen, Jennifer Quintin, and Roberta "Bobbe" Torgerson.

To the core of professional and master home bread bakers who guided my hands and taught me the techniques and significant recipes I still depend upon today: Ed Espe Brown, Marion Cunningham (for her taste critiques of my first loaves), baking instructor Diane Dexter, Barbara Hiken, Madeleine Kamman, Judy Larsen, Donna Nordin, Joe and Gayle Ortiz, Lou Pappas, Connie Pfiffer, Barbara Power, Tom Solis, and my very first beau ideals, David and Nancyjo Terres.

And to my favorite cooking school proprietors, who allowed me to hone my craft in public and often fire up the ovens for baking a multitude of test loaves: the Canos of San Francisco School of Cooking, the Classy Chef in Lafayette, Louise Fiszer (the exceptional equipment and props from her cookware shop grace the photography pages of *Bread*), Judith Dunbar-Hines, Mary Risley of Tante Marie's Cooking School, Martin and Susan Yan, and of course, my first efforts out of the bakery kitchen of Saint Michael's Alley Restaurant in Palo Alto, California.

Contents

The Craft of Baking Bread

BAKE BREAD A FEW TIMES A YEAR FOR FUN, creating a contemporary yet personal work of art. Bake bread once a month to celebrate holidays and to give as a gift a product of your own craftsmanship. Bake bread every week to incorporate whole grains and flours as a regular part of your diet. Whatever your needs, home baking is a simple, uncomplicated kitchen art. Lots of people who love to bake know that baking bread does not have to be a stressful task; it is a part of food preparation that feels good to the hands as well as to the soul.

Bread has become not only a topic of conversation; it has become *interesting.* A dying art is being revived. Look around: It's everywhere. Wonderful artisan-style regional bakeries are springing up to produce down-to-earth loaves rivaling homemade bread in quality and wholesomeness. For generations, American cities have had bakeries that provided all kinds of ethnic breads. New, young customers are now getting in line with loyal older ones. Old-time commercial wood-fired ovens, many shut down in the 1950s in the face of more efficient modern technology, are the rage, turning out *pains d'autrefois,* the rustic loaves of yesteryear. Such ovens are even being built in backyards for bread buffs in smaller, often more elaborate versions incorporating old heat-conducting materials like brick, adobe, and soapstone. The loaves they produce are substantial in size as well as full of flavor.

Restaurants heed their customers' requests for better bread, both elegant establishments and humble eateries. Dedicated bakers are turning out crusty low-fat, grain-sweet European-style naturally fermented loaves along with standard American favorites like orange-flecked baking-powder corn breads and old-fashioned hotel-style cream biscuits to fill the breadbasket. Brunches feature hand-rolled honey-wheat croissants and endless variations on French toast with thick slices of specialty breads. And since customers want to buy their favorite loaves to take home, many restaurants have added retail outlets.

Travelers have long journeyed to legendary French *boulangeries* and the bread counter of Harrod's food emporium in London for a quintessential crusty loaf, often in the hopes of reviving some of the wholesome, good-tasting bread of their childhood. Food magazines feature articles on breadmaking almost every month. High-fashion magazine food editors chronicle their travels in terms of what bread is eaten where and recount their attempts to recreate it at home. But some of the best bread available are the loaves you make yourself from simple recipes. You can heed a baker's fancy and create your own masterpiece that tastes good.

The sweet flavors of molasses and flowery honey, pungent garlic, aromatic seeds and spices, tangy dried fruits, rich nuts, cold-pressed oils and sweet creamery butter, and protein-rich grains are mixed with sea salt, pure water, and the ingredient that is at once mystical and practical—baker's yeast.

Every time you bake, the basic elements of earth, water, air, and fire come together. In Native American languages there is no word for artist, simply "one who is skilled" at some everyday task. And the function of such a person is defined as being a guide to how to combine the mediums of the inner and outer human world. Scoop grain from the earth; mix it with sea salt, pure water, and airborne wild yeasts; let the dough rise to form a minute airy mesh network; coil or roll it into a shape; and then expose it to the heat of fire's flame to create a beautiful, nourishing food. It is a lyrical blending of the elements.

The Apprentice Baker

WITH THIS MANUAL OF RECIPES, you have acquired an informal text and lesson guide to becoming a more proficient baker of yeast breads. You probably already have in mind the type of baker you wish to become. The practical material in this book will give you an opportunity to learn the foundations of baking as if you were taking a formal course of study in a vocational school or on-the-job training as an apprentice baker in a bakery or restaurant kitchen. This way, you will get to skip the years of washing dishes and floors and observing others before touching the dough that a traditional apprenticeship often entails. You will learn about assembling and mixing the ingredients, about kneading, forming the loaf, and placing it in the oven. You will learn about the properties of various flours and grains, what different ingredients add to a dough, of mixing methods, and how equipment works to form your loaf into your vision. You will experiment with your instincts about time and with temperature and with your hands in feeling what is right. You will develop your palate and raise your standards; you will learn the balance of a delicate touch and the authority to command the dough. People who have baked bread for years will also find something here—good recipes, often astonishingly so in view of their basic ingredients. The simple alchemy of flour, yeast, salt, and water becomes much more when fueled by your passion and hands-on involvement.

The instructional lessons in this book are set out step by step in an ascending scale of difficulty and proficiency, each building upon the others in theory and practice. New basic techniques will be very detailed and then subsequently described in the common language of a standard cookbook. Your progress as a baker will evolve with the manual repetition of the recipes, with applying the information presented with each lesson, and with reviewing your part in the technical process. If you repeat each recipe two or three times in succession, all the better.

For me, a basic bread book should be filled both with delicious and simple nourishing recipes that are easy to create and suitable for everyday eating and that utilize a variety of wholesome grains and with a few more complicated festive sweet breads. At the same time, the recipes must utilize the essential time-honored core techniques practiced by all yeast bakers. Most breads have a short, easy-to-assemble list of ingredients. Read each recipe through carefully before you begin working so as to visualize the process as a whole, then coordinate your kitchen work space, place your pantry in order, and assemble your equipment. That way, you will feel more composed than if you haphazardly try to pull together all the elements during the work phase. A clean, organized work space is as important as developing new skills. Cleaning up and greasing pans are as important jobs as mixing a dough. As you develop experience, the instructions that seemed complex will become obvious; steps will be more predictable, and your confidence, skill, and understanding will grow as well. Don't be discouraged. It is natural to be timid in handling the ingredients at first. Speed and accuracy in executing techniques are an acquired manual skill.

The mistakes you make should serve as the guideposts of your growing knowledge. Learn from them, rather than ignoring them or overcriticizing your work. Trial and error are the key to becoming a good baker. Every baker, no matter what the level of proficiency, has had to make them to learn about the feel of a kneaded dough or judge the correct volume in rising.

The basic principles not to be overlooked in any bread are accurate measurements, appropriate kneading and rising times, correct baking temperatures, and the right length of time in the oven. Carelessness and overbaking are equal sins in the bakery. Become familiar with the tools and equipment that are part of the job: mixers, bench scrapers, bread pans, wash brushes, and your oven. Become familiar with the raw materials and the crucial different steps in fermentation known as primary (the initial rise), secondary (an optional second rise), and tertiary (the rise after shaping in the mold, sometimes referred to as the panary stage). Only later should you work with ingredient variations of your favorite recipes to find new taste or texture combinations, like dried fruits, nuts, spices, and extract flavorings, that make your breads unique.

Utilize the principles that French food writer and culinary instructor Madeleine Kamman describes as the "trinity of the brain, heart, and hands," the innate intelligence coordinating your senses that comes into focus when an art is practiced. Gauge your doughs and loaves with all your senses: See what is a smooth dough or degree of brownness in a baking loaf; smell the strong aromas of raw yeast fermenting and the alluring scent of the finished loaf; hear that very distinctive hollow thump when tapping the surface or bottom of a loaf with your knuckle at the end of its baking; and finally, taste your loaf, a just reward for your efforts. Eye and nose appeal in a loaf are as important as the ingredients used in its composition. Exercise your judgment here. Baking is an essentially introspective process. This sensory base will be your starting point. This is the realm and language of the baker.

This book is based on my years as an instructor of baking as well as the successful recipes I've made since I first began baking. Keeping journals of all my classes has enabled me to share my understanding and knowledge of baking with you, even though we are not in a formal classroom situation and may never meet in person. I will share my views on the hows and whys along with the directions, so that you will have the benefit of learning as you work, rather like having "an angel on your shoulder." Become familiar with using the baking lexicon at the back of the book while working through the recipes; it is more efficient to under-stand and assimilate a few specialized terms intrinsic to baking while you are working. It is better if you follow the recipe to the letter the first time, leaving the experimenting and adjusting until later, as the smallest variation in a baking formula can produce a significant difference in the finished loaf. Your eventual modifications and adaptations will open up new paths of creativity. Breadmaking is a part artistic, part scientific endeavor, and you have embarked upon the journey.

Orientation

CONSIDER THE FOLLOWING LISTING as a new way of looking at an outline of yeast breadmaking. It is nothing more than a series of steps in a defined order, and it will become second nature to you. In some ways it is like learning a new language, but this one can easily be mastered by executing the basic sequential steps set down in each recipe. The recipes in this book all follow this outline, from the first pan loaf recipes focusing on the three indispensable basics—white, whole-wheat, and rye—to twisted egg breads, freeformed French and Italian breads and rolls, and dense whole-grain hearth breads. There are also an elementary flatbread and stuffed savory breads, a variety of soft rolls with their beguiling shapes, and finally, a repertoire of sweet yeast breads with fillings and simple icing finishes. At the beginning of each recipe, a timetable is given for the estimated length of time for each step to help you organize your work schedule. During the work process, you can refer to the section called The Baking Process (page 17) for answers to any questions that arise. The section on Special Techniques contains in-depth instructions for indispensable freezing and storage techniques. Before you know it, you will reach your end: serving and eating your own homemade bread. The following outline of sequential steps should help get you on your way.

1   Selecting a recipe and calculating preparation time

2   Assembling a work space, the equipment, and
    ingredients

3   Measuring the raw ingredients

4   Activating the yeast or preparing a sponge starter

5   Mixing—by hand, electric mixer, or food processor

6   Turning the dough out of the bowl

7   Kneading

8   First rise

9   Deflating the dough

10 Dividing and shaping the dough

11 Second rise

12 Preparing the oven

13 Baking

14 Cooling

15 Storage

Breadmaking Basics

The Baking Process

A YEAST DOUGH GOES THROUGH THE FOLLOWING PREDICTABLE SEQUENCE of changes no matter what type of ingredients, method of mixing, or shaping techniques are used. These steps are the key to controlling your product and to understanding the process of creating and baking a dough into a loaf.

- Forming carbon dioxide gases from a leavening, whether yeast, baking powder, or baking soda. Air is incorporated during the mixing and steam is created from the moisture in the dough during the heat of baking.
- Forming a mesh network to trap the expanding gases. Working the dough through kneading develops the proteins, or gluten.
- Forming the structure of the dough by setting the starches, a process called gelatinization. This occurs in the presence of heat, beginning at about 150°F. Structure is also set with the coagulation of the proteins. Correct baking temperature is important for these steps.
- Evaporation of moisture during baking through steam. One pound of raw dough will lose about 1½ to 2 ounces of moisture during baking. A brown crust is formed as moisture evaporates from the surface and the heat changes the chemical components of the starches, milk, and eggs. Sugar in the dough will make for a darker crust as it caramelizes.
- Melting the fats into the dough structure. This occurs at different temperatures, depending on what type of fat is used.

To transform a dough into a digestible product involves understanding temperature, applying an appropriate mixing method, working the dough by kneading, allowing for fermentation during the rising periods, and baking off the dough to form a loaf. These processes are described here in detail.

Temperature is a consideration throughout the entire process of mixing, kneading, rising, and baking bread. The first important step is to activate the yeast, which is the primary leavener in these breads. Yeast is a living organism and is very sensitive to temperature. When properly activated, it remains alive throughout the process of constructing a dough until it is killed in the heat of the oven during baking. It is activated in the conditions of moisture and food and in a narrow range of warm temperatures. Below 34°F, it goes into an inactive suspended state for storage or for refrigerating or freezing a dough for periods of time, and it dies at temperatures above 140°F. Maximum fermentation occurs between 75° and 90°F. The temperatures best for proofing doughs are, for slow action, 60° to 70°F, and for fast action, above 100°F. The only way to completely kill yeast is with too much heat. For the beginner, an instant-read yeast thermometer is invaluable here. The time-honored method is to drop some of the liquid on the inside of your wrist; if there is no sensation of either warm or cool, it is fine. Once activated in warm water with a bit of sugar for food, yeast lives about 15 to 20 minutes. For a longer period of activation it needs more food, or a host, such as flour. If the water is too hot, the yeast may be killed, in which case it will fail to foam; any dough made from it will not rise.

The mechanical action of mixing and kneading produces friction, which warms the dough. Under the most ideal conditions, temperature of the liquid, flour, and room will be the same. Pay attention to the weather. Since doughs are more active when it is warm and humid, use cooler liquid to slow the yeast action; I often use ice water (a professional trick widely used in hot climates) on very hot baking days. Initially the action will be slow, but it will increase as the dough warms naturally to room temperature.

Dissolving or proofing yeast

✻

Pour about ¼ cup warm water into a small bowl or cup. If using dry yeast, the thermometer should read 105° to 115°F, and the liquid should feel very warm to the touch but not hot. If using fresh yeast, the thermometer should read 80° to 90°F. Sprinkle 1 tablespoon dry yeast or crumble the .06 ounce cake of fresh yeast into the water. (Yeast is dissolved in 4 times the volume of water or other liquid.) Stir gently a few times with the handle of a small spoon or mini whisk to moisten evenly. Add a large pinch of sugar (a scant ⅛ teaspoon) or a few drops of honey, malt syrup, molasses, or maple syrup. (This mixture is sometimes referred to as a slurry.) Set the bowl or cup aside at room temperature. The spoon or whisk may be left submerged in the mixture if yeast has stuck to it. Within a few minutes the yeast will begin to bubble into a thick foam and double in volume. It is now ready to be added to a sponge starter or dough batter for further mixing. If no bubbling occurs, the yeast is inactive and should be discarded. Always check the freshness date when you purchase yeast and buy only quantities that will be used in a short period of time.

Mixing methods

❀

Two traditional and two modern methods are used to activate a batter and create a smooth yeast dough, activate gluten, and evenly distribute the yeast. The first and more traditional method involves mixing the yeast with a bit of sugar and a small amount of warm water and allowing it to stand a few minutes until it activates, or proofs. It is then mixed with all the remaining liquid and dry ingredients to form a dough. Most of the recipes in this book use this procedure, referred to as the plain-dough, direct or straight method. This may be done in a bowl or directly on the work bench, utilizing the ancient well method, in which the wet ingredients are mixed into the center of a mound of flour. More modern straight-dough methods include the rapid-mix method (also known as the one-bowl method and developed by the Fleischman Yeast Test Kitchen in the 1960s) suited to machine mixing in food processors and bread machines. Yeast and a portion of the dry ingredients are mixed with hot liquid, then the remaining flour is added to form the dough, with about 5 to 8 minutes total mixing time. When the mixing is done in a food processor, it takes about 1 to 2 minutes (page 31). In the refrigerator method (also known as CoolRise, page 28), the dough is mixed, kneaded, and shaped as directed in the recipe, then conveniently set in the refrigerator to rise from 2 to 24 hours.

Other recipes use the 2-step sponge method or 2-stage mixing method, which involves making an initial thin prefermentation starter batter. It is also the mixing method for making dough that utilizes a fermented piece of dough left over from a previous batch and for natural sourdough breads, which have a natural bacteria and wild yeast sponge starter. A sponge starter combines liquid with an equal amount of flour and fortifies it with a small amount of cultured yeast. This mixture forms a variety of consistencies, from semiliquid batter to a thick sticky mass that ferments as it stands at room temperature before the initial mixing of the bread dough. Doughs that are constructed from sponge starters are known for being easy to handle and having a firm yet supple consistency. The prefermentation begins the work of evenly distributing the yeast and moistening the gluten, the work that will be completed by hand during the kneading process.

A sponge can double in volume in 30 to 45 minutes, but different recipes call for the sponge standing anywhere from 2 to 4 hours. The traditional method for creating full-flavored, long-rise lean country loaves has prefermentation taking anywhere from 4 to 24 hours. The longer the sponge ferments, the more developed the flavor and the more irregular the inner crumb. Such variables as humidity and yeast quality are taken into consideration. Some sponges are allowed to just rise; others rise and fall back upon themselves. Salt is never added to a sponge starter, as it can inhibit the growth of the yeast. A sponge will sometimes

❀

A lean dough is low in fat and sugar. European country breads, French and Italian breads, and pizza, as well as pita, lavash, chapati, naan, rusks, matzo, pretzels, and bread sticks are lean-dough breads.

A rich dough has more fat and sugar in varying amounts. American pan loaves, soft dinner rolls, sweet rolls, crumpets and English muffins, coffee cakes, and brioche are rich-dough breads.

Rolled dough includes croissants, which contain no sugar, and Danish pastries, which do. They have layers of dough and fat, which are incorporated by a rolling and folding method.

be substituted for the first rising period. These breads also have an increased shelf life and give a boost to low-gluten flours.

Any yeast bread recipe can be made at home by hand or in a heavy-duty electric stand mixer with any of these interchangeable methods. The difference is not in the quality of bread but in the time it takes to handle it. The hand method generally takes about five vigorous minutes to knead properly what the electric mixer will do in one; the food processor requires a few kneads after the machine has done its work.

MIXING A YEAST DOUGH BY HAND

Proof the yeast in warm water according to recipe directions and add it to the rest of the wet ingredients in a large heavy mixing bowl. If a sponge has been made, incorporate it at this time. Using a large balloon whisk, add 1 cup of flour and the salt into the wet mixture, mixing about 1 to 3 minutes to create a smooth and creamy batter; as the mixture thickens with the continuing addition of flour ½ cup at a time, switch to a wooden spoon when the whisk becomes clogged. Always add flour in ½ to 1 cup increments, beating vigorously to completely incorporate the flour between additions. The dough will gradually firm up and become a shaggy mass that clears the sides of the bowl. This is the signal that the dough surface has absorbed enough flour and is ready to be scraped out onto the flour-dusted work surface and be kneaded.

MIXING A YEAST DOUGH WITH A HEAVY-DUTY ELECTRIC STAND MIXER

Proof the yeast in warm water or construct a sponge according to recipe directions and place directly in the bowl. Use the whisk attachment to mix. Place the rest of the wet ingredients in the mixer bowl. On low speed (speed 2), add 1 cup of flour and the salt to the wet mixture, mixing about 1 minute to create a smooth and creamy batter. Continue to add flour ½ cup at a time. As the mixture thickens, switch to the flat mixing paddle attachment on the KitchenAid or to the dough hook on the Kenwood and other models when the whisk becomes clogged. (I do not use the KitchenAid dough hook because it does not clear the sides of the bowl properly.) Add the flour slowly on the lowest speed, then finish mixing the dough mass on medium (speed 4/5). The dough will form in 1 to 3 minutes of mixing, slowly working its way up the paddle to become a shaggy mass that clears the sides of the bowl, unless the texture is otherwise described in the recipe. This is the signal that the dough surface has absorbed enough flour and is ready to be scraped out onto the flour-dusted work surface and kneaded by hand. The dough is usually more moist on the top than at the bottom of the bowl. Do not scrape out the very dry bits—they will stay dry bits in the dough. The KitchenAid dough hook can be attached at this point to knead the dough ball, but I don't recommend it in the early stages of mixing because it cannot remove the lumps. Use only heavy-duty models of electric mixers; doughs can burn out weaker motors. High speeds are never used for mixing yeast doughs. For making a yeast dough in a food processor see page 31.

Kneading

❋

Kneading thoroughly mixes the ingredients, distributes the yeast, releases the gases produced by the growing yeast, and strengthens the moistened gluten strands to a springy elasticity. Turn out the shaggy mass of dough onto a lightly dusted work surface (only 2 to 4 tablespoons of flour, depending on the consistency of your dough batter). A plastic or metal dough scraper, also known as a bench scraper, is invaluable for manipulating the dough if it is still a bit sticky at this point. Kneading incorporates fresh oxygen into the dough, which is important to the rising and to the finished shape of the loaf. Lean doughs as well as doughs made entirely from high-gluten bread flour are kneaded longer and more vigorously than rich doughs. A few minutes of practice is really all anyone new to kneading needs to get the feel of a springy dough. For detailed directions on kneading techniques, refer to the first recipe in this collection, White Mountain Bread (page 40).

A soft dough, such as that for batter breads, yeast coffee cakes, brioche, or other breads containing a large proportion of fat, requires an exact measure of flour, tends to be sticky, and may not be able to retain its shape without a mold. Chilling the dough is often required for satisfactory handling.

A medium dough, such as that for sweet doughs and whole-grain breads, will just hold its shape yet be smooth. The moisture in these doughs is important for a moist, tender, light-textured bread. While being kneaded, whole-grain doughs will have a definitely tacky, even grainy or nubby quality. The dough should not be worked beyond this point.

Rolled dough, such as for Danish pastry and croissants, undergo a double leavening process with a well-chilled yeast and egg dough and a folding technique that creates delicate layering when the moisture in the butter evaporates during baking.

A stiff dough is firm and smooth and begins to have a slightly unyielding yet resilient tension. All-white-flour doughs are in this category. Whole-grain doughs kneaded to this point will be dry and crumbly when baked.

FOUR BASIC STEPS
FOR
KNEADING DOUGH.

Rising

❋

Rising, also referred to as fermentation period or proofing, allows the gluten to become smooth and elastic. The dough changes from a firm, heavy mass to a large, puffy one. Peeking is allowed! Rising times vary with the temperature of the dough (the temperature of the ingredients all affect this), its richness, the surrounding atmospheric conditions, and the amount and kind of flour and yeast used. The surface of the dough is greased lightly, to allow for easy stretching as it swells, and covered loosely—the yeast needs to rise effectively—to prevent drying. High humidity and high altitude cause bread to rise faster. In these cases, reduce the rising time. Cold slows down the process (see Where to Put Dough to Rise, below). The longer the rise, the better the flavor and texture, but the dough should not be allowed to rise higher than 2½ or 3 times its volume. If the dough must be left for more than 3 hours, it may be deflated and refrigerated to prevent overrising and the breaking of the strands of gluten. Generally, a dough with a tablespoon or cake of yeast and two cups of liquid rises in 1 to 3 hours, with each subsequent rise requiring about half the initial time. Doughs can be rushed by adding more yeast, but take care not to add too much or an unsavory strong flavor will prevail, or by using moist heat to 90°F (placing the rising container in a pan of hot water). An overfermented dough, also referred to as an old dough, is sour tasting; an underfermented dough, also referred to as a young dough, is coarse in texture and flat looking. Letting the dough have its time to ripen is the best. Rich sweet doughs and rye doughs low in gluten are shaped into loaves while young. Lean doughs rise double to triple in bulk; rich doughs are best when not quite doubled.

If a recipe calls for a double or triple rising of the dough before it is shaped, all the better. It can be allowed to rise several times with no problem as long as it is deflated as soon as it reaches the full rise. Deflating the dough—not punching it down—is necessary to release the trapped carbon dioxide. In case your dough overrises and collapses, knead briefly, form the loaf, and bake immediately.

TO DETERMINE IF A DOUGH IS PROPERLY RISEN

Press two fingers deeply into the puffy dough, removing them quickly. If the depression remains, the dough is ready; if it fills in quickly, allow more time for rising.

WHERE TO PUT DOUGH TO RISE

The ideal room temperature for even rising of American-style breads is 75° to 80°F. Just position the container of dough in a protected spot. European and CoolRise loaves rise at lower temperatures, around 70° to 75°F. To speed up a dough on cold days, use such places in the kitchen as near the pilot light of a gas range (use a glass or crockery container since metal can cook the delicate surface of the dough and plastic might melt), in the oven of a gas range with the pilot light on, or on top of the refrigerator. The back seat of a car parked in a sunny spot is another good place.

TO USE A MICROWAVE OVEN TO RISE A DOUGH

This is known as the micro-rise method. Be certain your microwave oven has a low enough setting so as not to kill the yeast.

Place an 8- to 12-ounce glass of water in the back corner and microwave on high until steaming, about 5 minutes. Move to the rear of the oven. Reset the oven to its lowest power (10 percent). Place the kneaded dough in a lightly oiled large microwavesafe bowl, turning once to grease the top. Or, if your microwave is large enough, leave the dough in the workbowl. Place the bowl in the oven and cover loosely with plastic wrap. Heat the oven at intervals of 2 to 5 minutes, letting the dough rest undisturbed for 5 minutes in between until the dough has doubled in bulk, about 15 to 20 minutes for compressed and active dry yeast, and 10 to 15 minutes for instant and quick-rise. Remove the bowl from the oven and deflate. Shape as directed. The shaped loaves may be risen before baking in microwavesafe glass pans for 5 to 8 minutes in the same manner.

TO DEFLATE A DOUGH

Fold over the sides of the dough into the center and press down. Place the dough upside down in the rising container. This keeps the dough at an even temperature, releases carbon dioxide, introduces fresh oxygen, and helps develop the gluten.

TO DETERMINE IF A DOUGH IS RISEN ENOUGH TO BE PLACED IN THE OVEN

Cut off a small piece of dough (the size of a lime) during the shaping. Place the dough ball in a bowl of mildly tepid water at room temperature. When the ball floats to the top, the dough has risen sufficiently to be placed in the oven.

Baking

Normally ovens are preheated before baking, unless otherwise directed for the cold-oven method. The proper temperature provides the heat necessary for the best oven spring, or final expansion of the dough. During the first ten minutes of baking, the last gasp of the expanding yeast produces this oven spring, and the gluten strands stretch to contain the gases. The smell is of evaporating alcohol. What happens is this: Baking stops the yeast fermentation at 140°F and coagulates the proteins in the gluten and eggs at 165°F. The starch begins to swell at 130°F, transferring moisture; alcohol evaporation begins at 175°F, creating steam and trapping the by-products in the baked dough. Fats and sugars melt into the dough and the starch changes into dextrins to create a brown crust. If the loaves were underrisen, the baked loaf will be small and compact. If overrisen, the bread will collapse when the gluten strands break in the oven. A break on the side occurs when the bread continues to rise after the top crust has set. This can be prevented by scoring the bread before baking.

Circulation of air between pans is imperative for proper baking, so place the pans at least 2 inches apart in the middle of the oven, unless otherwise directed, or staggered on 2 shelves. Avoid placing pans directly above or below each other as this would block the heat.

Baking times vary according to the size and density of a loaf and the amount of butter and sugar in it. As a general reference for baking, lean doughs, such as French and Italian breads, bake at high temperatures, 400° to 425°F; pizzas bake at the highest setting on a home oven, about 500°F; an American-style loaf and whole-grain breads bake at 350° to 375°F; dinner rolls bake at 375°F; and rich sweet doughs and rolls bake at a moderate 350°F (to prevent overbrowning in standard home electric or gas ovens). The heat of professional roasting, deck, and convection ovens is more intense and needs to be adapted by experimentation for the best results.

Alternatives to the standard method of baking include baking in the microwave oven and in a bread machine. Since both methods are so different from using a conventional oven, it is important to consult a microwave or bread machine cookbook or the manufacturer's instructions and use recipes and proportions specifically developed for those appliances.

TO CHECK DONENESS BY THERMOMETER

This method is especially useful for rich doughs, which do not sound hollow when tapped and are usually tested by inserting a cake tester. Insert an instant-read thermometer into the bottom of the bread. Breads are thoroughly baked at 190°F. A loaf has not finished baking until it is completely cool. Loaves stop baking in the oven at about 212°F, when all the moisture has evaporated.

Storing homemade bread

The best homemade bread is eaten within 8 hours of baking. Although loaves begin staling as soon as they are removed from the oven and exposed to the air, after a few hours they lose that wonderful fresh-baked aroma and become drier due to the loss of moisture. The science of staling is one long studied by professional bakers and many products are often added to bread to retard it, like soy flour, raisins, ground spices, or barley malt syrup. Sourdough starters also retard staling. Wrapped breads stale faster than unwrapped ones—remember the old-fashioned breadbox?—moist breads stale faster, and lean doughs are completely stale after 24 hours. The crust stales at a different rate than the interior crumb.

For optimal short-term storage, place completely cooled loaves in moisture-proof bags at room temperature or in an old-fashioned breadbox. The exception here is for hard-crusted, fat-free peasant-type breads, which are best eaten the day they are made or frozen, as the crusts will soften as they absorb moisture from the interior crumb and become leathery-textured. Refrigeration accelerates a different—and quick—type of staling by drawing the moisture out of bread much faster than at room temperature and changing the structure of the starch. This type of staling is stopped by freezing and can be reversed by reheating. Refrigeration is a must, however, for specialty breads with perishable ingredients like cheese or other dairy products where you want to avoid rancidity.

TO FREEZE BAKED BREAD

The best way to store bread for more than a few days with very little loss of taste, texture, and nutrition is to freeze it. Wrap fully baked and fully cooled loaves first in plastic, then in a layer of aluminum foil (to prevent freezer burn), or a double layer of reusable zip-style plastic freezer bags. The loaves must be completely cool, which takes about 4 hours; otherwise, the center will freeze solid and defrost into a soggy mass. Label and date the packages. Freeze up to three months in a freezer, less in the freezer compartment of the refrigerator since it is not a true deep freeze.

Defrost loaves at room temperature for at least 3 hours in their wrappings, shaking out any accumulation of ice crystals. Unwrap and reheat at the temperature at which they were baked for about 8 to 10 minutes. Breads may be refreshed, or thawed, in a 325°F oven for 20 to 40 minutes, or until heated through. If the bread is unwrapped, the crust will crisp. Rolls are best reheated wrapped since they tend to dry out more quickly than loaves. Sliced bread may be refreshed instantly in a toaster. Serve immediately.

TO FREEZE BAKED SWEET BREAD

Cool to room temperature, wrap, and store as for other breads. Glaze, ice, or dust with powdered sugar, if called for in the recipe, after thawing and reheating, just before serving.

TO REHEAT HOMEMADE BREAD IN A STANDARD OVEN

Place the whole unsliced loaf, wrapped in aluminum foil, on the center rack of a preheated 350°F oven for 15 to 20 minutes, to crisp the crust and heat into the center. Sliced breads and dinner rolls are also best reheated wrapped in foil to retain moisture. The old method of placing bread or rolls in a dampened brown paper bag and warming them in a preheated 350°F oven until the bag is dry is still one of the best ways to refresh day-old bread. Just be certain the bag has not been made from recycled material, which is toxic.

TO REHEAT HOMEMADE BREAD IN A MICROWAVE OVEN

Place unwrapped bread or sweet rolls on a paper towel. Microwave on high only until just warmed, about 15 seconds. Overheating will toughen the texture.

❁

Type of Bread	Refrigerator	Freezer
Lean and rich egg breads		
Baked pan and country loaves	—	3–4 months
Unbaked dough	1–2 days	3–4 weeks
Brioche		
Baked	—	3–4 months
Unbaked dough	2–3 days	3–4 weeks
Sweet breads and coffeecakes with fillings		
Baked without icing	—	2–3 months
Unbaked dough	2–3 days	2–3 weeks
Stuffed savory breads		
Baked loaves	—	1 month
Unbaked dough	1–2 days	
Pizza and focaccia doughs		
Baked bread with toppings	—	1 month
Unbaked dough	1–2 days	3–4 months
Danish pastries and croissants		
Shaped, unbaked dough	8–12 hours	1–2 weeks
Unbaked rolled dough	2–3 days	2 weeks
Baked without icing	—	3–4 months
Soft dinner rolls		
Shaped, unbaked	8–12 hours	1–2 weeks
Baked	—	3–4 months
Unbaked rich dough	2–3 days	
Yeasted waffles and pancakes	—	3 months
Yeast and Flour		
Yeast		
Granulated active dry	6–8 months	1 year
Fresh compressed	2–5 weeks	
Flours and meals	4–6 months	1 year

❁

Special Techniques

MANY LITTLE TOUCHES CONTRIBUTE TO THE BASIC CONSTRUCTION of bread doughs, bringing the loaf to life by adding flavor, aroma, color, and texture. Knowledge of these special techniques for handling and storing ingredients, converting to other methods of mixing, and shaping doughs can make all the difference.

Freezing dough

Raw doughs are more perishable than baked doughs, but they also may be frozen—after mixing and kneading or after shaping—with excellent results. Some bakers add a bit more yeast to the recipe if planning on long storage to compensate for some loss of activity. Place the kneaded dough, well oiled, immediately in a freezer bag, leaving some space for the swelling that will naturally occur while the dough freezes solid. Shaped dough can also be placed in disposable aluminum loaf pans and frozen in the same manner. Place shaped freeform loaves or dinner rolls on a nonstick disposable aluminum pan, or on a parchment-lined baking sheet that will fit into the freezer. Cover tightly with plastic wrap and freeze until firm. Remove the frozen rolls to plastic freezer bags. After freezing, squeeze out any excess air and tightly seal. Store for about 3 to 4 weeks or up to 2 months if you have a very efficient freezer.

TO DEFROST FROZEN DOUGH

Defrost the dough at room temperature for about 4 to 6 hours (rolls take 2 to 3 hours) before you want to work with it, or let it defrost in the refrigerator for 12 to 24 hours, until almost doubled in bulk. Frozen dough can also be defrosted in a microwave oven: Place the frozen dough in a greased microwavesafe bowl or glass loaf pan and microwave at the lowest power setting (10 percent) for 15 minutes, turning the bowl or pan a quarter turn every 4 to 5 minutes if you do not have a carousel. Follow the directions for a second proofing in a well-oiled container, shaping and baking as directed in the recipe.

Refrigerator doughs

Refrigerating dough is also referred to as the CoolRise method. It retards the yeast activity. Any yeast dough can be refrigerated at different times in the rising process to fit in with your time schedule. A dough may be made one day and baked the next. The chilling temperature (ideally about 45°F) retards the action of the yeast; when the temperature is allowed to come back to room temperature or warmer, the dough comes out of its suspended state to continue rising. Sweet doughs rich in fat and milk keep the best (there is some fat and sugar to feed the slowed yeasts), and can be refrigerated for up to 4 days; lean doughs made with water and little or no sweetening can be refrigerated for up to 2 days. Potato breads, soft roll doughs, sweet rolls, and coffee cakes are excellent made in this manner.

HOW TO STORE REFRIGERATOR DOUGHS

Mix and knead the dough according to recipe instructions. After kneading or deflating the dough after one of its rising periods, place the dough in a deep bowl or plastic container, leaving room for the dough to expand to triple in bulk, if necessary. Brush the surface completely with melted butter or oil to prevent a crust from forming. Cover tightly with plastic wrap and refrigerate. The dough will rise slowly as the internal temperature drops, so it may need to be deflated every 2 hours until thoroughly chilled. When ready to use, deflate the dough and let stand at room temperature until risen to double in bulk, as cold dough is not easy to shape. This may take 4 to 6 hours, varying with the type of dough and temperature. Shape, rise, and bake as directed in the recipe.

HOW TO STORE REFRIGERATOR DOUGH LOAVES OR SHAPED ROLLS

Let the kneaded dough rest on the work surface, loosely covered with plastic wrap, for about 30 minutes. Divide and shape the dough as stated in the recipe. Use pans that can take fast changes in temperature, such as metal or disposable aluminum, rather than glass or clay. Cover the pans with the loaves or rolls with plastic wrap, loose enough to allow for dough expansion. Refrigerate for 2 to 24 hours. As the internal temperature drops, the dough will continue to rise, to about 1 inch above the rim of the pan. Remove it from the refrigerator to bake at any time. Let the pans stand at room temperature while preheating the oven to the specified temperature for 20 minutes. The dough will still be cold as it goes into the oven. Glaze, score, and bake as directed in the recipe.

❀

Although bread is usually baked in pans or formed into round, oval, or long shapes, there are times when only a specially shaped loaf will do. It might be a shape traditionally associated with a holiday or a long square loaf that can be cut into square slices for sandwiches, the so-called Pullman loaf. The following directions tell how to form three of the simplest—and most versatile—shapes. For other special shapes, see the variations following House French Bread (page 64–68).

TO SHAPE A BRAIDED CROWN LOAF

This braided wreath shape works best with egg-rich doughs, such as the Jewish Egg Bread (page 50) topped with sesame seeds. Gently deflate the dough, turn out onto a clean work surface, and divide into 3 equal portions. Roll each section into a smooth, thick rope about 25 inches long. Roll back and forth under your palms to even the thickness. Lay the ropes side by side lengthwise and, beginning at the middle, braid together. Turn the dough around and braid the other side from the middle. This makes for an even braid. Holding the two ends, pinch together and tuck any excess under. Place on a greased or parchment-lined baking sheet. Adjust the braid so that it is an even circle; there does not need to be a large hole in the center. Cover loosely with plastic wrap and let rise until almost doubled in bulk, 30 to 40 minutes. Because of the eggs, this loaf does not need to double completely; it will rise a lot in the oven. Glaze, decorate, and bake as directed.

TO SHAPE A TURBAN LOAF

This coil shape works especially well with egg-rich doughs. Deflate the dough, turn out onto a clean work surface, and divide into 2 equal portions. Roll each section into a smooth, thick strip about 30 inches long, with one end about 2 to 3 inches fatter than the other. Roll back and forth with your palms to lengthen and taper the thinner end. Leave the fat end on the work surface and lift the tapered end. Wind the rest of the dough around the center section 2 to 3 times, forming a compact coil. Pinch the end to flatten and tuck it under securely. Place the coil on a greased or parchment-lined baking sheet or in a 9-inch springform pan. Repeat with the second strip. Cover loosely with plastic wrap and let rise until almost doubled in bulk, 30 to 40 minutes. Because of the eggs, this loaf does not need to double completely; it will rise a lot in the oven. Glaze and bake as directed.

TO SHAPE A PULLMAN LOAF

A Pullman pan has a sliding top so that the dough is enclosed on all 4 sides to form a perfectly square loaf. The loaf is generally made for its easy, even slicing for sandwiches. The bread is characterized by a dense, even crumb and hairline crust. This type of mold works well with American-style yeast breads. Deflate a

❀

risen dough made with about 5½ to 6 cups of flour and pat into a 10-by-15-inch rectangle on a clean work surface. Roll up tightly from the long edge, jelly-roll fashion, and pinch the seam to seal. Place, seam side down, in a well-greased 11-by-5-inch Pullman pan, or divide the cylinder in half and place in two 9-by-5-inch Pullman pans. The pan should be no more than one-third to one-half full. Cover with plastic wrap and let rise at room temperature until the pans are filled four-fifths full, about 45 minutes. Slide the cover onto the pan. If using regular loaf pans, use a metal baking sheet, with one side greased, to cover the dough; weight the baking sheet with a brick. Bake in a preheated oven as directed in the recipe for 25 minutes. Remove the lids and bake another 15 to 20 minutes, or until the bread is browned and solid to the touch. Remove immediately from the pans to cool completely on a rack before slicing.

Simulating a baker's deck oven

❁

A baker's deck or brick oven is unique in that it allows loaves to be baked directly on the hot firebrick or hearth surface, often with pressurized steam injection for extra moisture during baking. The very hot surface makes for high oven spring and a crisp crust by quickly pulling the moisture from the surface of the dough; it bakes breads in a fashion similar to country hearth breads. The best way to reproduce the interior of these type ovens is to use baking stones or unglazed ceramic tiles to produce a steady, radiating heat. Use commercial pizza stones sold in gourmet shops, kiln shelves from a pottery supply, or 1½-inch-thick refractory bricks, that is, unglazed 6-inch-square high-fired quarry tiles. Commercial pizza stones are available in two round sizes, 12 inches and 16 inches in diameter, or as a 12-by-14-inch rectangle. The hot bricks kit is a 16-inch-square aluminum tray supporting eight terra-cotta tiles.

Line the lowest rack of your home oven with a baking stone, bricks or tiles (laid closely together), or commercial hot bricks kit. Leave 2 inches of air space all the way around the tiles and the oven wall to allow for heat circulation. A tip from an Italian home baker is to place a second layer of tiles on the topmost shelf of the oven. Breads may be shoveled onto the hot stones with a peel or baked in pans (not glass) directly on the tiles. Avoid placing doughs that drip butter or sugar directly on the stone's porous surface; the drips burn quickly and will produce a bitter smoke-filled oven and stains that cannot be scrubbed clean.

❀

La Cloche is an unglazed clay baking dish with 2-inch sloping sides and a domed cover. It is useful for baking a large crackly-crusted country loaf, but high-sugar doughs tend to stick mercilessly, so avoid baking them in it. To use La Cloche, sprinkle the dish with flour, cornmeal, semolina, or farina, and place the dough ball in the center of the dish. Move the dough around to cover the bottom and up the sides a bit. Using a serrated knife, slash the top surface decoratively, no more than ¼ inch deep. Cover with the domed cover and let rest at room temperature for 15 minutes. Preheat the oven to 400°F. Before placing the baker in the oven, remove the cover and rinse the inside of it with tap water, draining off excess drips, but do not dry (this moisture creates steam during baking). Place back over the slightly risen dough ball and place in the pre-heated oven.

Bake in the center of the oven for 30 minutes. Remove the bell with heavy oven mitts to allow the loaf to brown thoroughly. Continue baking for 15 to 20 minutes, or until the bread is golden brown, crisp, and sounds hollow when tapped. Carefully remove the loaf from the oven with heavy oven mitts and transfer it to a rack to cool for 15 minutes before serving warm. To clean La Cloche dish, tap out the excess flour and scrub off any stuck-on bits with a brush and water only. Do not use soap, which can impart a taste to the next baked loaf.

Converting recipes for mixing in the food processor

❀

Check your manufacturer's instructions; some processors have a motor too weak for bread dough. Small processors can handle about 3 cups of flour and half as much liquid. A larger processor can handle 6 to 7 cups total of flour and 2½ cups of liquid. Tepid or cold liquid is used, except for proofing the yeast, as the fast action of the motor can overheat a dough quickly. Since doughs can become overworked quickly, follow the time instructions for mixing and kneading exactly, setting a timer if necessary. The following recipe is adapted for your convenience from House French Bread (page 63) and may be used as a guide for adapting other recipes in this book.

❀

House French Bread Made in the Food Processor

PROOFING THE YEAST: In a small bowl, combine ¼ cup warm water (105° to 115°F), 2 teaspoons active dry yeast, and 1 teaspoon granulated sugar. Stir to dissolve and let stand at room temperature until foamy, about 10 minutes.

MIXING THE DOUGH: In the workbowl of a food processor fitted with the metal blade, place ¾ cup semolina flour, 2½ cups unbleached flour, and 1½ teaspoons salt. Pulse 6 times to combine. With the processor running, add 1¼ cups tepid water (100°F), slowly pouring it through the feed tube. The dough will form a ball that cleans the sides of the bowl. Process dough ball about 45 seconds.

CONSISTENCY ADJUSTMENT AND HAND KNEADING: Test dough and adjust the consistency by adding more flour, 1 tablespoon at a time, if the dough is very sticky or water if there are dry bits around the bowl. Process 15 seconds longer. Remove dough from the workbowl and place on a lightly floured work surface. Gently knead by hand just to form a smooth ball, about ten times (I always give a few kneads by hand to feel and even out dough consistency). Proceed to rise, form, and bake as in basic recipe (page 63).

Converting recipes for mixing in the electronic bread machine

❊

Any yeast bread recipe may be adapted to the mix and bake cycles of an electronic bread machine. Follow the manufacturer's instructions and recipe guidelines for your model; each one has its idiosyncrasies. The recipe booklets accompanying most models include many very good plain and specialty bread recipes with appeal to a wide range of home-baking needs.

Once the basic recipe has been mastered, start substituting and experimenting, with the original recipe serving as your guide. The loaves will be shaped according to the mixing cylinder—oval, cubed, or a high rectangle reminiscent of English cottage pan loaves. Every loaf has the distinctive mark of the automatic bakery, with a bottom hole created by the kneading paddle. The entire process takes about 3 to 4 hours, unless programmed otherwise.

- Once the machine cycle is set and running, do not change the settings.
- Most bread machines have the capacity for 1 cup of liquid and 3 cups of flour, which means dividing most traditional yeast bread recipes in half. The loaf will be approximately 1½ pounds when baked. This total amount of flour includes any other dry ingredients such as bran, whole wheat flour, oatmeal, and other specialty flours.
- If your model does not have a cool cycle to remove the warm, moist air at the end of the baking cycle, remove the loaf from the pan as soon as possible and cool on a rack.
- The best bread machine loaves are made with a high proportion of high-gluten bread flour; this helps to ensure a loaf that is not too dense. Many people add a few tablespoons of gluten flour to offset heavier specialty flours.
- Layer the ingredients so that the yeast and dry milk are in the bottom of the baking cylinder. They must not touch the liquid, especially during delayed cycles.
- All bread machine models require the use of active dry or instant yeast, which do not need preliminary fermentation.

Adapting yeast measurements when multiplying recipes

❁

To prevent overrising and too yeasty a flavor, increase the amount of yeast by one-third when doubling or tripling a bread recipe. For example, a recipe that calls for 1 tablespoon active dry yeast will take only 4 teaspoons when doubled or 2 tablespoons when tripled.

Substitutions for granulated sugar

❁

Many bakers prefer honey, molasses, or maple syrup to granulated sugar in yeast doughs, because they add flavor, color, and softness. To substitute honey or maple syrup for sugar, use ¾ cup of honey or maple syrup for every cup of granulated sugar and reduce the measurement of the liquid ingredients by ¼ cup for each cup of sugar listed in the recipe. To substitute molasses, use half of the measurement of sugar called for in the recipe and reduce the measurement of the total liquid ingredients by ⅓ cup for each cup of sugar. To substitute brown sugar, use 1⅓ cups brown sugar for every cup of granulated sugar.

❁

Flavored sugars are fragrant additions to doughs or toppings for sweet breads. Prepared ahead, they allow the baker to have a choice in the pantry for convenient use.

VANILLA SUGAR

Vanilla is the fruit pod of an orchid widely cultivated in Madagascar, which is marketed as Bourbon vanilla, Tahiti vanilla, which is more flowery in flavor, and Mexican vanilla (similar to but milder than Bourbon vanilla). It is a principal aromatic ingredient in sweet yeast doughs and fillings. To make vanilla sugar, bury a piece of whole or split vanilla bean with its skin peeled back in 2 cups sifted powdered sugar in an airtight container. Let stand for 4 days to 2 weeks until scented as desired. Use the sugar in place of regular sugar in sweet dough recipes. Replace the sugar as needed, not the bean, although the bean should be replaced when it dries out. The same method may also be used with granulated sugar. Vanilla sugar keeps indefinitely, covered tightly, at room temperature.

CINNAMON OR CASSIA SUGAR

Cinnamon sugar is essential as an accent spice, in traditional swirled rolls and loaves, or as a topping. True cinnamon is the seductively-flavored dried bark of a cultivated shrub grown primarily in Sri Lanka, Madagascar, Brazil, Japan, and the West Indies. Cassia has a stronger flavor—the one most Americans are accustomed to. It is grown in southern China and northern Vietnam. Different cinnamons vary in strength, color, aroma, and flavor. A blend of 2 tablespoons ground cinnamon or cassia for 1 cup of granulated sugar makes a mild yet flavorful cinnamon sugar, but it may be mixed to taste. Ground nutmeg or cardamom may also be used in the same way. Cinnamon sugar keeps indefinitely, covered, at room temperature.

ROSE PETAL SUGAR

As long as wild or hybrid roses are unsprayed and pesticide-free, they may be used as a delicate accent flavor for special occasion sweet breads. Prepare the rose petals by placing the whole rose head in a bowl of cool water. Drain and dry on layers of paper towels or in a salad spinner. Using kitchen shears, cut the petals off above the white base tip attached to the stem and bottom center of the flower; the base tip is bitter. Use 2 cups sifted powdered sugar to 1 heaping cup of rose petals. Place about ½ cup of the powdered sugar in the bottom of an airtight container. Lay a third of the dry rose petals on top of the sugar. Continue to layer sugar and petals 2 more times, ending with a layer of sugar. Cover tightly and let stand at room temperature for 1 week before using. Flower-flavored sugars will keep for about 3 months. Sift before dusting on top of breads after baking. Scented geraniums, lavender blossoms, and calendula petals may also be used as a flavor enhancer.

❁

LEMON SUGAR

Use unsprayed fresh lemons (I use the tangy Meyer variety). Three tablespoons of lemon sugar will approximately equal the freshly grated zest of 1 large lemon. Using a small paring knife or vegetable peeler, peel off the zest of 6 large lemons, leaving the pithy white on the lemon. Place the zest in a food processor with ¼ cup granulated sugar. Pulse to grind fine. Add 1¼ cups more granulated sugar and squeeze some lemon juice over the sugar to moisten slightly; mix quickly to evenly combine the lemon sugar. Store in a covered jar in the refrigerator up to 2 months.

Storing and preparing nuts

Nuts are often referred to as a pure and innocent food, as they come in their own protective wrapping with naturally built-in nutrition and nourishment. They add a unique character and flavor to bread doughs from the high percentage of natural fat that is absorbed into the dough during the heat of baking. Use shelled raw nut pieces, toasted, or ground nuts in both sweet and savory loaves. Almonds and hazelnuts, unlike walnuts and pecans, have thin skins which can be removed before using. Store all shelled nuts in the refrigerator for about nine months or in the freezer for no longer than 2 years. They can turn rancid quickly at room temperature.

TO TOAST ALMONDS, PECANS, WALNUTS, AND OTHER NUTS

Toasting gives nuts a richer flavor and crisps the texture. Slivered or sliced nuts will toast much quicker than pieces or halves.

IN A CONVENTIONAL OVEN: Place the nuts on an ungreased baking sheet on the center rack of a preheated 325°F oven for about 10 to 15 minutes, depending on the size, stirring once. The nuts will be hot and very pale golden. Do not bake until dark in color or the nuts will taste burnt. Cool to room temperature before using in a bread dough.

IN THE MICROWAVE OVEN: Place the nuts in a single layer on a shallow paper plate or double layer of paper towels. Toast nuts on high power for about 3 to 4 minutes per ½ cup, stirring every 1 to 2 minutes to prevent burning and facilitate even browning. This method toasts nut very quickly, so watch carefully!

IN A SKILLET: When a recipe calls for ¼ cup or less of toasted nuts, they can be toasted in a heavy skillet on the stove top. Place whole or chopped nuts in a dry skillet over low heat. Stir constantly or shake the pan until the nuts are slightly colored and aromatic, 2 to 4 minutes. Remove from the pan to cool.

TO GRIND NUTS

Ground nuts are used as a replacement for part of the flour. Use a European-style hand nut grater, electric blender, or food processor fitted with the metal blade and be sure the nuts are dry. Add 1 to 2 tablespoons of sugar or flour during the grinding to absorb the nut oil and prevent the formation of a paste. Properly ground nuts have a powdery, fluffy quality. Lightly spoon into a measuring cup.

TO BLANCH ALMONDS

Fill a medium saucepan three-quarters full of water and bring it to a boil. Add the whole shelled almonds and remove the pan from the heat. Let stand for 3 minutes. Immediately rinse the nuts under cold running water. Squeeze the nut kernel out of its loosened brown layer of skin by holding the nut between your thumb and index finger. Let the nuts dry on a layer of paper towels for at least 2 hours.

TO SKIN AND OVEN-DRY PISTACHIO NUTS

Put the nuts in a heatproof bowl and pour boiling water to cover over them. Let nuts stand for 1 minute, then drain. Turn nuts out onto a dish towel and rub off skins. Dry nuts on a baking sheet in a preheated 300°F oven for 10 minutes. Store in an airtight container in the freezer.

TO TOAST AND SKIN HAZELNUTS OR FILBERTS

These nuts have a tough, loose skin that is first removed by toasting. Place hazelnuts in 1 layer in a baking pan. Toast in a preheated 350°F oven for 10 to 15 minutes, shaking occasionally, or until they are lightly colored and the skins blister. Wrap nuts in a dish towel and let them stand for 1 minute. Rub nuts in a towel to remove the skins. Let cool.

TO MAKE ALMOND MILK

When prepared with water, almond milk is a unique lactose-free liquid in bread dough. Use ¼ cup almonds to 1 cup of boiling liquid. Combine the nuts and boiling water or milk in a food processor and process until an emulsion is formed. Add ¼ teaspoon almond extract per cup of almond milk and let steep 30 minutes. Pour the milk through several layers of cheesecloth placed over a bowl. Refrigerate or freeze until needed.

Cutting dried fruit

Place the dried fruit on a cutting board. Sprinkle a bit of flour from the recipe onto the fruit and chop with a chef's knife. Kitchen shears work well when sprayed with a nonstick vegetable spray. Chopping dried fruit may also be done in a food processor fitted with the metal blade; add a bit of flour to prevent clumping.

Plumping dried fruit

❁

When dried fruits are added to bread doughs they will not soften further during the rising and baking. It is therefore better to soak the fruit in a warm liquid before adding to the dough. Soak dried fruits for at least 10 minutes and as long as one hour before adding them to a dough. You can use hot water, wine, a liqueur that has a complementary flavor of the bread, or fruit juice to restore moisture, soften, and add flavor. If the fruit is very hard, simmer gently in the liquid for about 10 minutes. Do not cover the fruit while plumping; excess sulphur dioxide, used to preserve color and freshness, needs to evaporate.

Adapting a traditional bread recipe for special diets

❁

Yeast breads may be easily adapted to address a variety of food allergies. Following are some suggested substitutions for ingredients.

EGGS

Use egg replacers, which are free from egg, dairy, soy, gluten, and corn products, following the package instructions. If you are allergic only to egg yolks or are on a cholesterol-free diet, use Eggbeaters or another commercial egg substitute, following the package instructions, or use all egg whites in place of whole eggs. The substitution ratio is 2 egg whites for each whole egg.

SUGAR

Replace sugar, honey, maple syrup, and other sugars with fructose or a commercial sugar substitute, following the package instructions. Fructose is 60 percent sweeter than sucrose, so less will be needed if it is substituted for regular sugar. Fruit juice concentrates and fresh fruit purées are also good alternatives for other liquid sweeteners.

SALT

Use light salt or a commercial salt substitute to replace all or some of the salt.

LACTOSE INTOLERANCE

Use a commercial product available in health food stores, such as NutQuik powder (from almonds), Lacto-Free, Tofu White (soy based), or dry goat's milk powder. Soy- and rice-based liquids are also available, or make your own almond milk (page 36) to be used in place of regular milk.

GLUTEN INTOLERANCE

Wheat and rye are the only grains that contain gluten. For each cup of wheat flour, substitute a combination of ⅔ cup brown rice flour, ¼ cup potato starch or soy flour, 2 tablespoons tapioca flour (cassava flour) or nut flour, and 1 teaspoon xanthan gum, a dried microorganism important for a chewy loaf when gluten is missing (available at natural food stores). This formula is just a starting suggestion for eliminating gluten and proportions may be adjusted for your personal palate, but keep in mind that the brown rice flour is the important base flour. Gluten-free breads are best mixed in a heavy-duty electric mixer, since the doughs can be quite dense, and baked in small or miniature loaf pans for even baking. They may also need a bit more liquid added during the mixing stage to avoid a dry baked loaf. Other gluten-free flours and grains are cornmeal, corn, buckwheat, barley, teff, and bean flours, as well as millet, oats, and arrowroot powder.

Recipes

White Mountain Bread

Bread made in a loaf pan using unbleached white flour in the straight-dough mixing method is the most popular type of soft-crusted sandwich bread made in the continental United States today. Before you wince at the thought of a basic white bread, consider that this homemade loaf made with milk, butter, and honey bears little resemblance to the packaged sliced varieties commonly available. The secret here is in the flour. Use a good brand of unbleached all-purpose or bread flour for the best results. Brands vary, so make each batch with a different brand of white flour, especially if you are using organic or stone-ground white flour from small mills, until you find the one you like the best. The combination of water and milk makes for an exceptional crumb. This is the perfect loaf of homemade bread with an appealing, slightly fermented aroma. It is especially good for buttered toast and sandwiches. This recipe is written in a detailed step-by-step format that will act as a learning guide for subsequent recipes made in this style. Although this dough may be made in a heavy-duty standing electric mixer, I recommend you make it by hand the first time, if possible, to feel how a dough is formed during all stages of mixing.

BAKING TIME 40 TO 45 MINUTES

¾ cup warm water (105° to 115°F)

1 tablespoon (1 package) active dry yeast

Pinch of granulated sugar

1½ cups milk (105° to 115°F)

3 tablespoons unsalted butter, melted, or vegetable oil

3 tablespoons honey

1 tablespoon salt

6 to 6¼ cups unbleached all-purpose or high-gluten bread flour

1 PROOFING THE YEAST AND ASSEMBLING THE INGREDIENTS: In a small bowl or 1-cup liquid measuring cup, pour ¼ cup of the warm water. It will read between 105° and 115°F on a thermometer. It should feel very warm to the touch but not hot. Sprinkle the yeast and the pinch of sugar over the surface of the water. Stir gently a few times with the handle of a small spoon or mini whisk to moisten evenly. (It is okay to leave the spoon or whisk submerged in the mixture if a lot of yeast has stuck to it. This mixture is sometimes referred to as a slurry.) Let the bowl or cup rest at room temperature (75° to 80°F) for about 10 minutes. Within a few minutes the yeast will begin to bubble into a thick foam and double to triple in volume. If you wish to slow this stage of proofing, use a lower temperature water, about 80° to 100°F. While the yeast is proofing, assemble the rest of the ingredients and equipment on your work surface. Set your mixing bowl, whisk, wooden spoon, measuring cups and spoons, and dough scrapers, or heavy-duty electric mixer, if using, on the center of the work surface. Place the flour at the side of the work surface for easy access during the kneading.

2 MIXING THE DOUGH: In a large bowl using a whisk or in the bowl of a heavy-duty electric mixer fitted with the paddle attachment, combine the remaining water, milk, butter or oil, honey, salt, and 1 cup of the flour. Beat hard until creamy, about 3 minutes by hand or 1 minute in the mixer. Stir in the yeast mixture. By hand or on low speed in the electric mixer, add the remaining flour, ½ cup at a time (to allow for thorough incorporation), until a soft dough is formed which just clears the sides of the bowl. Switch to a wooden spoon when necessary if making by hand. The dough will be slightly stiff and sticky.

3 KNEADING: Turn the dough out onto a lightly floured (about 2 tablespoons to start) work surface with the plastic dough scraper to prevent the dough from sticking to the work surface. Often the dough will be moist on top and have dry bits on the bottom. The goal is to change the dough manually from a rough, shaggy mass into a smooth, malleable one by allowing the dough to absorb a bit more flour and create a stretchy structure. Use the plastic scraper to begin the first kneads, if desired, dusting with flour only 1 tablespoon at a time, just enough as needed to prevent sticking. Begin by folding the top edges in halfway toward you. Push away with the heels of the hands and then give the dough a quarter turn to keep the area to be worked directly facing you. As you pull back, use your fingers or the scraper to lift the farthest edge of the dough and fold it back toward you to lay it over itself, and push again, allowing the dough to slide across the work surface where it will absorb the flour it needs. Repeat the pushing, turning, and folding sequence, developing a comfortable pace and rhythm and observing the dough as well as feeling it firm up under your hands. Dust with flour as needed. The dough will start out quite soft, requiring gentle motions, then firm up as you work. It will very quickly become smooth when your hand is brushed across the surface and springy when a finger is poked into the top. Turn the dough over to look for tiny blisters evenly distributed just under the surface; these indicate that gas bubbles have been trapped and incorporated. The surface that is being worked will have a crease. Too little flour and the dough will have sticky spots, too much and the dough will become stiff and hard to work. Adding too much flour is the most common problem with beginning bakers, so as soon as the stickiness is gone, stop kneading. Knead until smooth and springy, a total of 1 to 3 minutes for a machine-mixed dough, since the mixer has begun the kneading process with vigorous mechanical action, and 4 to 7 minutes for a hand-mixed dough, to allow for mixing in additional flour. Each batch of dough is unique and presents minor variables in time.

4 FIRST RISE: Place the dough in a deep container, crockery, or glass mixing bowl lightly greased by brushing with vegetable oil, mild olive oil, or melted butter. (I favor a plastic container with straight sides that encourage the dough to rise up instead of out and flat.) Turn the dough once to coat the top so that the plastic wrap does not stick and the surface does not form a crust. Cover completely with a piece of plastic wrap, laying it over loosely rather than tight around the sides. This leaves room for expansion if it's needed. Note on the container where the dough will be when risen to the desired volume. Let rise at room temperature until double in bulk, about 1½ to 2 hours. The age-old test is to press a fingertip into the top of the dough to see if the indentation remains. If it needs to rise more, the indentation will fill back in quickly. Do not worry or rush the dough if it takes longer. The dough may be refrigerated at this point, covered tightly with a double layer of plastic wrap, for up to 18 hours, if desired. See page 28 for handling and baking off refrigerator loaves.

5 SHAPING AND SECOND RISE: Turn the dough out onto a lightly floured work surface to deflate. Lightly grease the bottom and sides of two 9-by-5-inch loaf pans. Without working the dough further, divide it into 2 equal portions with a metal scraper or knife. The scraper requires a swift downward motion to cut, while the knife uses a gentle sawing motion to avoid tearing. To shape a pan loaf, pat each portion of dough into a long, rough rectangle. It does not need to be exact. Fold the dough into thirds, overlapping the 2 opposite ends in the middle. Beginning at the short edge, tightly roll up the dough jelly-roll fashion into a log that is about the same length as your pan. Pinch the ends and the long seam to seal. While placing the loaf into the pan, tuck the ends under to make a neat, snug fit. The log should be of an even thickness and fill the pans about two-thirds full. Cover loosely with plastic wrap and let rise again at room temperature until the dough is fully double in bulk and about 1 inch over the rims of the pans, about 45 minutes.

6 BAKING OFF AND COOLING: Twenty minutes before baking, preheat the oven to 375°F. Remove the plastic wrap and, using a serrated knife, with the quick motion of your wrist make a long slash lengthwise down the center of the loaf, no more than ¼ inch deep, to create a long groove that will spring open. This is a decorative design, but it also gives the dough room for expansion. Immediately place on the center rack of the oven and bake 40 to 45 minutes, or until the loaves are golden brown in color and the sides slightly contract from the pan. Lift one end of the loaf out of the pan to peek underneath to check for an even browning on the bottom, and tap on the top and bottom with your finger; it should sound hollow. If the bottom crust is too pale, remove the loaf from the pan and place it directly on the rack for 5 more minutes or continue baking in the pan in the lower third of the oven for 5 minutes and check again. Remove the loaves from the pans immediately by holding the pan with a thick dish towel or insulated oven mitt and guiding the loaf out. Gently set each loaf on its side on a wire or wood cooling rack. For proper cooling, air must circulate all around the loaf, so leave plenty of room between the loaves and at least 1 inch of space under the rack to keep the crust from getting soggy. Be sure to let the loaves rest for at least 15 minutes, to allow excess moisture to evaporate so the center will not be doughy and to finish the baking process. Loaves are best slightly warm or at room temperature.

Baker's Notes Every recipe lists an approximate amount of flour rather than an exact measure, since variables such as humidity and the type of flour affect the amount of liquid the flour will absorb during mixing and kneading. ◆ Sometimes your liquid will be too cool and the dough slightly chilled. Set the oven thermostat on the lowest setting and preheat for 15 minutes. Place the dough in a medium mixing bowl and rub the top with a thin layer of oil to prevent a crust from forming. Turn off the oven heat and let the dough rest for 15 minutes in the oven. Check every 5 minutes thereafter until the dough slightly warms and is more malleable. Do not leave it too long or it will begin to bake on the surface. ◆ In the case of a dough that is too warm, which can happen on a hot day, place the dough in a medium mixing bowl, rub the top with a thin layer of oil to prevent drying, cover with plastic wrap, and place in the refrigerator for up to 1 hour. ◆ When baking off your loaves, resist opening the oven door during the first 15 minutes in the oven, which is when the dough reaches its maximum rising height due to the rapidly rising internal temperature, known as oven spring. This gives the structure time to set. Other than that, your loaf will not suffer from slight changes in temperature as would a cake, it will only take longer to bake. ◆ For maximum protection for your hands, wrists, and lower arms, use heavy-duty oven mitts, such as the ones designed for barbecuing. ◆ White Mountain Bread may also be made into 2 round loaves or a Pullman shape (page 29–30).

Storage

White Mountain Bread has a good shelf life and does not stale quickly, staying moist about 3 days. Store the unsliced bread wrapped in a plastic food storage bag at room temperature, or freeze (see page 25).

Specific Skills

◆ Measuring. ◆ Cleaning special equipment, such as pans and hand tools. ◆ Care and selection of ingredients. ◆ Introduction to temperature considerations. ◆ Preparing a yeast slurry. ◆ Mixing a straight dough. ◆ Introduction to kneading techniques. ◆ Deflating a dough. ◆ Observing the different stages of fermentation. ◆ Forming a pan loaf. ◆ Slashing the top of bread decoratively. ◆ Arranging the pans properly spaced on the oven rack.

Cinnamon Swirl

Cinnamon bread is probably the simplest yet at the same time most popular American sweet breakfast bread a baker can make. It can be made from many different bread doughs, including roll doughs, that vary in richness or type of grains used and amount of cinnamon in the filling. This is my version of the old favorite. Use a really good grade of ground cinnamon or cassia for a distinctive flavor. Cinnamon bread may be baked in a variety of pans and shapes (pages 29–30).

BAKING TIME 40 TO 45 MINUTES

1¼ cups warm water (105° to 115°F)

1 tablespoon (1 package) active dry yeast

Pinch of granulated sugar

1 cup warm milk (105° to 115°F)

6 tablespoons (¾ stick) unsalted butter, melted

½ cup granulated sugar

1 tablespoon salt

2 eggs

7½ to 8 cups unbleached all-purpose or high-gluten bread flour

Spice Filling

⅔ cup (packed) light brown sugar or granulated maple sugar

2 tablespoons ground cinnamon

3 tablespoons unsalted butter, melted

1 PROOFING THE YEAST: In a small bowl or 1-cup liquid measuring cup, pour in ¼ cup of the warm water. Sprinkle the yeast and the pinch of sugar over the surface of the water. Stir to dissolve and let stand at room temperature until foamy, about 10 minutes.

2 MIXING THE DOUGH: In a large bowl using a whisk or in the bowl of a heavy-duty electric mixer fitted with a paddle attachment, combine the remaining water, milk, melted butter, sugar, salt, eggs, and 2 cups of the flour. Beat hard until creamy, about 1 minute. Stir in the yeast mixture. Add the remaining flour, ½ cup at a time, until a soft, shaggy dough that just clears the sides of the bowl is formed. Switch to a wooden spoon when necessary if making by hand.

This is a bread with a tight, honeycombed texture, hairline swirl pattern, and even crumb that is creamy in color. It easily holds its shape when sliced, even when warm. It has a high-domed deep golden crust over the entire loaf and a spicy aroma. The best toast!

Equipment
Small and large (at least 6-quart) mixing bowls
Measuring spoons and cups
Large balloon whisk and wooden spoon
Heavy-duty electric mixer with flat paddle attachment or dough hook (optional)
Plastic and metal dough scrapers
Dough container, preferably a 6-quart deep plastic container
Rolling pin
Pastry brush
Serrated knife for scoring
Cooling rack

Baking Pans and Yield
Two loaves using standard 9-by-5-inch metal, nonstick, glass, or disposable aluminum loaf pans, greased on all inside surfaces. If using glass or black-finish aluminum pans, reduce heat by 25°F.

Baking Temperature
350°F

Timetable
Total preparation time About 4 hours
Working time 15 minutes
Kneading time About 5 minutes
First rise 1 to 1½ hours
Shaping time 5 to 10 minutes
Second rise 40 minutes

Storage

Cinnamon Bread has a good shelf life and does not stale quickly, staying moist about 3 days. Store the unsliced bread wrapped in a plastic food storage bag at room temperature, or freeze (see page 25).

Specific Skills

◆ Preparing an elementary egg-enriched straight dough.
◆ Filling, rolling up, and sealing the swirl. ◆ Introduction to sugar-spice fillings.

3 KNEADING: Turn the dough out onto a lightly floured work surface with a plastic pastry scraper and knead until soft and springy, 1 to 3 minutes for a machine-mixed dough and 4 to 7 minutes for a hand-mixed dough, dusting with flour only 1 tablespoon at a time, just enough as needed to prevent sticking. The dough will be smooth and springy but not dry.

4 FIRST RISE: Place the dough into a lightly greased deep container. Turn the dough once to coat the top and cover with plastic wrap. Let rise at room temperature until double in bulk, about 1 to 1½ hours. In a small bowl, combine the sugar and cinnamon until loose and evenly distributed. Set aside.

5 SHAPING AND SECOND RISE: Turn the dough out onto a lightly floured work surface to deflate. Lightly grease the bottom and sides of two 9-by-5-inch loaf pans. Without working the dough further, divide it into 2 equal portions, using a sharp edge. Roll or pat each portion of dough into a rough 9-by-12-inch rectangle of even thickness. Make sure there are no holes in the dough. Brush each piece with 1 tablespoon of the melted butter. Sprinkle each with half of the cinnamon-sugar, leaving a 1-inch border all the way around the edges. If you desire a topping, reserve 1 to 2 tablespoons of the cinnamon-sugar at this time. Beginning at the short edge, roll up the dough jelly-roll fashion into a tight log. Pinch the ends and the long seam to seal. This is to prevent the sugar from leaking out while baking. Place the loaves, seam side down, in the loaf pans. Brush the tops with the remaining melted butter and dust lightly with cinnamon or the reserved cinnamon-sugar, if desired. Cover loosely with plastic wrap and let rise at room temperature until the dough is fully double in bulk and about 1 inch over the rims of the pans, about 40 minutes.

6 BAKING OFF AND COOLING: Twenty minutes before baking, preheat the oven to 350°F. Using a serrated knife, make 3 diagonal slashes across the top of the loaf, no more than ¼ inch deep. Place the pans on the center rack of the oven and bake for 40 to 45 minutes, or until the loaves are golden brown, the sides slightly contract from the pan, and the loaves sound hollow when tapped with your finger. Remove the loaves from the pans immediately to a cooling rack. Loaves are best slightly warm or at room temperature.

Baker's Notes Loaves containing sugar in the dough or filling bake at a lower temperature than those without. ◆ Hot loaves should be removed immediately from the pans to avoid the bread sticking to the pan. ◆ I like to use the disposable aluminum baking pans for the easiest cleanup, as the sugar can leak and stick to the pan. ◆ This recipe makes four 7-by-3-inch loaves. ◆ The filling may be embellished by sprinkling each loaf with ¼ to 1 cup of golden or dark raisins, dried currants, dried blueberries, or dried cherries, all plumped in hot water for 10 minutes, drained, and dried on paper towels. ◆ In lieu of the cinnamon-sugar topping, sprinkle with pearl sugar (page 149), or a Powdered Sugar Glaze (page 119). Dusting with flavored powdered sugar (pages 34–35) is an attractive and flavorful touch for special occasions.

Caramel Rolls

After cinnamon bread, the spiraled cinnamon roll is a pinnacle of home baking. It just cannot be made as good commercially. I learned this recipe from my friend Judy Larsen and have taught it in all my basic baking classes with unparalleled success. The dough is a simple straight dough that is risen once before being filled and shaped into pan rolls, which are more square than free-standing spirals. The dough is a bit richer than for soft rolls but leaner than for traditional sweet doughs. The rising time is also much shorter than for a butter-heavy traditional sweet yeast dough. Although any of these doughs work up into nice buns, I prefer this one. The spiral shape retains its form perfectly during the oven spring and baking. In Step 6 I have included instructions for refrigerating the formed rolls for convenient bake off early in the morning, allowing the baker to serve hot sweet rolls without any extra work time for breakfast.

BAKING TIME 30 TO 35 MINUTES

Dough

2½ cups warm water (105° to 115°F)

2 tablespoons (2 packages) active dry yeast

½ cup granulated sugar

1 egg

1½ tablespoons pure vanilla extract

⅓ cup vegetable oil

½ cup nonfat dry milk or buttermilk powder

1 tablespoon salt

7½ to 8 cups unbleached all-purpose flour

Caramel

1 cup (2 sticks) unsalted butter

2 cups (packed) light or dark brown sugar

½ cup light corn syrup

¼ cup water

Cinnamon Filling

6 tablespoons (¾ stick) unsalted butter, melted

1½ cups (packed) light or dark brown sugar

¼ cup ground cinnamon

1 cup chopped pecans

1 cup dried currants

Appearance

A large rectangle mass of pull-apart pan rolls with a fluffy top surface and tight, even creamy texture accented by the brown-spice swirl. The top surface is light brown and the bottom surface coated with caramel sauce, which thickens upon cooling.

Equipment

Small and large (at least 6-quart) mixing bowls

Measuring spoons and cups

Large balloon whisk and wooden spoon

Heavy-duty electric mixer with flat paddle attachment or dough hook (optional)

Plastic and metal dough scrapers, rubber spatula

Dough container, preferably a 6-quart deep plastic container

Small skillet

Rolling pin

Pastry brush

Serrated knife for slicing dough roll

Cooling rack

Baking Pans and Yield

Twenty-four large rolls using two 9-by-13-inch baking dishes, four 8-inch cake or springform pans, or two 12-inch ovenproof skillets, with sides greased and bottoms lined with parchment (optional).

Baking Temperature

350°F

Timetable

Total preparation time About 3 hours, longer if dough is refrigerated

Working time 15 minutes

Kneading time About 5 minutes

First rise 1 to 1¼ hours

Shaping time 10 to 15 minutes

Second rise 45 minutes

1 PROOFING THE YEAST: Into a small bowl or 1-cup liquid measuring cup, pour in ½ cup of the warm water. Sprinkle the yeast and a pinch of the sugar over the surface of the water. Stir to dissolve and let stand at room temperature until foamy, about 10 minutes.

2 MIXING THE DOUGH: In a large bowl using a whisk or in the bowl of a heavy-duty electric mixer fitted with a paddle attachment, combine the remaining water, the remaining sugar, egg, vanilla, oil, dry milk powder, salt, and 2 cups of the flour. Beat hard until creamy, about 1 minute. Stir in the yeast mixture. Add the remaining flour, ½ cup at a time, until a soft, shaggy dough that just clears the sides of the bowl is formed. Switch to a wooden spoon when necessary if making by hand.

3 KNEADING: Turn the dough out onto a lightly floured work surface with the plastic pastry scraper and knead until soft and springy, 1 to 3 minutes for a machine-mixed dough and 4 to 7 minutes for a hand-mixed dough, dusting with flour only 1 tablespoon at a time, just enough as needed to prevent sticking. Leave the dough moist and soft, yet at the same time smooth and springy.

4 FIRST RISE: Place the dough in a lightly greased deep container. Turn the dough once to coat the top and cover with plastic wrap. Let rise at room temperature until double in bulk, about 1 to 1¼ hours. In a small bowl, combine the sugar and cinnamon. Set aside.

5 MAKING THE CARAMEL: Prepare the caramel glaze 10 minutes before forming the rolls. Grease the sides and bottom of the baking pans or skillets, or grease the sides and line the bottom with parchment. In a small skillet or heavy saucepan, melt the butter, brown sugar, corn syrup, and water over low heat, stirring constantly. When melted, remove from heat. Immediately pour into the molds, dividing the amount equally. Spread evenly over the bottom with a rubber spatula. Set aside.

6 FORMING AND FILLING THE ROLLS: Turn the dough out onto a lightly floured work surface and divide it into 2 equal portions. Roll or pat each portion into a 12-by-15-inch rectangle. Leaving a 1-inch border all around the edges of the rectangle, brush the surface heavily with melted butter, then sprinkle evenly with half of the brown sugar, the cinnamon, pecans, and currants, in that order. Roll up jelly-roll fashion, starting from the long edge, and pinch the seam to seal. With a serrated knife using a gentle sawing motion, or a metal dough scraper using an even downward motion, cut each roll into 12 equal portions, each 1 to 1½ inches thick. Place the slices close together in the baking molds, spiral cut side down. Cover loosely with plastic wrap and let the rolls rise at room temperature for 45 minutes, or until puffy and even with the rims of the pans.

CUTTING THE
FILLED
DOUGH ROLL.

The rolls can be refrigerated or frozen before this last rise, retarding the dough for bake off at a later time. Cover the pans loosely with plastic wrap and refrigerate for 2 to 24 hours. Remove the pans to room temperature and let rest 30 minutes while preheating the oven. If freezing, use a disposable aluminum pan to avoid freezer burn or breakage. To thaw and bake off frozen rolls, let stand, uncovered, at room temperature until doubled in bulk, about 6 hours.

7 BAKING OFF AND COOLING: Twenty minutes before baking, preheat the oven to 350°F. Bake the rolls in the center of the oven until the tops are brown, 30 to 35 minutes. Remove from the oven and let stand 5 minutes on a wire rack. Place the cooling rack on top of the pan and, securely holding the hot pan with oven mitts, invert the pan on top of a plate or baking sheet. Take care not to touch the hot caramel. Let cool for at least 20 minutes, then pull apart to serve warm.

Baker's Notes All-purpose flour is used, rather than bread flour, as the blend of hard and soft wheat flours makes for the most tender sweet roll. ◆ Raisins, dried blueberries, dried cherries, or chopped dried prunes can be substituted for the currants. ◆ As a guide, yeast dough portioned out for one 9-by-5-inch loaf of bread will make up into 12 sweet rolls and 1 small coffee cake. ◆ Rolls can also be formed into a variety of shapes after filling: For a butterfly-like twin bun, cut the spiral a second time across the center almost through to the bottom and fan it open. For a rosette, with scissors held directly above the flat side of the cut roll, snip a cross almost to the bottom; 4 peaks will open during oven spring. For a basket, press a thin rolling pin into the center of the flat side of the cut roll to cause the layers of dough to spread out to either side. For double swirl buns, roll up the layered dough from either side to meet in the middle before cutting, rather than in jelly-roll fashion.

Storage
Cool Caramel Rolls completely to be reheated the next day. Store wrapped in plastic in the refrigerator. For longer storage, wrap in plastic and then in a layer of aluminum foil to freeze for 4 to 6 weeks.

Specific Skills
◆ Forming and cutting spiral rolls. ◆ Preparing caramel. ◆ Turning the rolls out of pans. ◆ Refrigerator doughs.

Appearance

A three-strand braid with a thin, glossy, deep-brown crisp crust and fine, even texture. The un-baked egg-rich dough is remarkably soft and silky in texture, with a pale, translucent quality due to the eggs. The bread is rich and cakelike, with a delicate flavor. It should be cooled before being cut to retain texture.

Equipment

Small and large (at least 6-quart) mixing bowls
Measuring spoons and cups
Large balloon whisk and wooden spoon
Heavy-duty electric mixer with flat paddle attachment or dough hook (optional)
Plastic and metal dough scrapers
Dough container, preferably a 6-quart deep plastic container
Pastry brush
Cooling rack

Baking Pans and Yield

Four loaves using standard 9-by-5-inch metal, nonstick, glass, or clay loaf pans, greased on all inside surfaces, or 4 medium freestanding braids using 2 parchment-lined 11-by-16-inch baking sheet pans. If using glass or black-finish aluminum pans, reduce heat by 25°F.

Baking Temperature

350°F

Timetable

Total preparation time About 5¼ hours
Working time 25 minutes
Kneading time About 8 minutes
First rise 2 to 2¼ hours
Second rise 1 to 1¼ hours
Shaping time 5 to 10 minutes
Third rise 40 minutes

Jewish Egg Braid

Time to master a classic. Jewish Egg Braid, traditionally known as challah, is a rich white flour loaf leavened with a high proportion of eggs paired with yeast. There are three rises and a short prefermention time to develop the subtle flavor. This recipe comes from my friend Ilana Sharum's Russian great-grandmother; it was translated for me from cursive Hebrew. The dough is mixed by hand using the old-fashioned well method, using a bowl rather than directly on the work surface. It is said that when you make this traditional bread every Friday, you are creating an atmosphere not just food. If you made only this bread for decades, you would still be hailed as an excellent baker. A must for any holiday dinner or celebration, the egg bread can be sculpted and baked up perfectly into a variety of intricate shapes, including a turban (page 29), a triangle or Tricorne (page 67), an oversized braid, a braided crown (page 29), oval loaves topped with a string of five balls, or stacked tiers of different sized braids. It makes excellent morning toast, a fine French toast, and is good for grilled sandwiches.

BAKING TIME 40 TO 45 MINUTES

About 7½ cups unbleached all-purpose flour
2½ cups warm water (105° to 115°F)
2 tablespoons (2½ packages) active dry yeast
⅓ cup plus 1 tablespoon granulated sugar
3 eggs
½ cup vegetable oil
2 teaspoons salt
Rich Egg Glaze (page 118)
2 tablespoons sesame or poppy seeds (optional)

1 MIXING THE DOUGH: In a large bowl, place 6 cups of the flour. Make a well in the center with your hand and pour ½ cup of the water into the center. Sprinkle the yeast and 1 tablespoon of the sugar over the water. Stir gently to dissolve (a bit of flour will also be incorporated) and let stand 15 minutes. Add the remaining sugar, remaining water, eggs, oil, and salt to the well and mix with a large wooden spoon or your hand with the fingers outstretched until a shaggy mass of dough is formed. Add the remaining flour, ½ cup at a time. The dough will form a ball and pull away from the sides of the bowl. This dough comes together quickly, so long mixing is unnecessary. The dough can also be mixed in the bowl of a heavy-duty electric mixer fitted with a paddle attachment.

2 KNEADING: Turn the dough out onto a lightly floured work surface with the plastic pastry scraper and knead by folding, stretching, and pulling until soft and springy, 5 to 8 minutes, dusting with flour only 1 tablespoon at a time, just enough as needed to prevent sticking. The dough will be smooth and springy but not dry.

3 FIRST AND SECOND RISE: Place the dough in a lightly greased deep container. Turn the dough once to coat the top and cover with plastic wrap. Let rise at room temperature until double in bulk, about 2 to 2¼ hours. Do not allow the dough to rise over double, as it has a tendency to tear and the baked loaf will not be as full-volumed as it can be. Gently deflate the dough with your fist, re-cover and let rise again until doubled in bulk, about 1 to 1¼ hours.

4 SHAPING AND THIRD RISE: Turn the dough out onto a lightly floured work surface to deflate. Lightly grease the bottom and sides of the 9-by-5-inch loaf pans or line the baking sheets with parchment. Without working the dough further, divide the dough into 4 equal portions. Further divide each portion into 3 equal portions. Roll each section under your palms into a rope that is tapered at each end. Gently dust the work surface with flour to lightly coat each rope (this keeps the shape more distinct during rising). Be sure the ropes are of equal size and shape. Place the 3 ropes parallel to each other. Begin braiding, starting in the center rather than at the ends for a more even shape. Take one of the outside ropes and fold it over the center rope, then repeat the movement from the opposite side. Continue by alternating the outside ropes over the center rope. When completed, turn the dough around and repeat the procedure from the middle out to the other end. Adjust or press the braid to fix any irregularities. Tuck the ends under and set into the loaf pans or pinch the ends into tapered points and place the loaves on the baking sheet for free-standing loaves. Brush the tops with some of the egg glaze. Cover loosely with plastic wrap and let rise at room temperature until the dough is almost double in bulk and about 1 inch over the rims of the pans, about 40 minutes. This bread needs only a three-quarter proof before baking; if longer, it can collapse during baking.

5 BAKING OFF AND COOLING: Twenty minutes before baking, preheat the oven to 350°F. Brush the surface of the loaves a second time with the egg glaze and sprinkle with seeds or leave plain. Place the pans on the center rack of the oven and bake 40 to 45 minutes, or until the loaves are deep golden brown, the sides slightly contract from the pan, and the loaves sound hollow when tapped with your finger. Remove the loaves from the pans immediately to a cooling rack. Loaves are best slightly warm or at room temperature.

Baker's Notes Many egg bread recipes, especially ones from Europe, use only egg yolks in the dough, rather than the whole egg. This is because yolks are capable of producing a bit higher volume than whole eggs, probably a technique left over from a time when yeasts were more unreliable than today. Substitute 1 whole egg for 2 yolks. ◆ Eggs contribute richness, greater volume, structure-building protein, and increased shelf life. Oil is added to counteract the tendency of egg breads to dry out quickly. ◆ Do not let the egg glaze drip down into the sides of the pan or the bread will stick. ◆ This recipe can also be shaped as plain rectangular loaves, 1 or 2 large freeform braids (check the size of your oven first) for celebrations, 3 spiral turbans (page 29), or 2 large braided crown wreaths (page 29). ◆ This basic recipe can be dressed up nicely with 1 to 2 cups of chopped dried fruit and/or nuts, candied peels, grated cheese, or ¼ cup chopped fresh herbs. ◆ Make a Cinnamon Egg Bread by rolling and coating the ropes in ground cinnamon before shaping the braid.

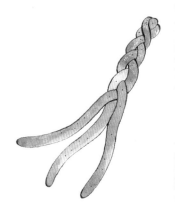

BRAIDING
THREE STRANDS
OF DOUGH.

Appearance

This is a bread with a soft texture and even crumb; it is matte white in color. It easily holds its shape when sliced, even when warm. The bread has a characteristic earthy umber-hued soft crust over the entire loaf.

Equipment

2-quart saucepan
Potato ricer or food processor
Small and large (at least 6-quart) mixing bowls
Measuring spoons and cups
Large balloon whisk and wooden spoon
Heavy-duty electric mixer with flat paddle attachment or dough hook (optional)
Plastic and metal dough scrapers
Dough container, preferably a 6-quart deep plastic container
Pastry brush
Serrated knife for slashing
Cooling rack

Baking Pans and Yield

Two loaves using standard 9-by-5-inch metal, nonstick, glass, or clay loaf pans, greased on all inside surfaces, or 24 pan rolls using a 10½-by-14½-inch roasting pan, preferably with a nonstick coating, or a parchment-lined 9-by-13-inch glass baking dish. If using glass or black-finish aluminum pans, reduce heat by 25°F.

Baking temperature

375°F

Timetable

Total preparation time About 3½ hours
Working time 30 minutes
Kneading time About 5 minutes
First rise 1 to 1½ hours
Shaping time 5 to 10 minutes
Second rise 45 minutes

Poppy Seed–Potato Bread

Probably one of the most popular of American farmstead breads, potato bread is made with mashed potatoes rather than with potato flour or starch. It has a superior flavor and a unique soft, fluffy crumb that lends itself well to preparing rolls as well as loaves. The yeast thrives on the starch in the potatoes, so the volume of the finished dough is high. The minute black seed of the opium poppy adds a crunchy, nutty texture and light, spicy flavor. Be certain to purée the potatoes well; any lumps will stand out in the finished loaf.

BAKING TIME 40 TO 45 MINUTES FOR LOAVES, 25 TO 30 MINUTES FOR ROLLS

1 large (8 ounces) russet baking potato
3 cups water
1½ tablespoons (1½ packages) active dry yeast
1 tablespoon granulated sugar
6½ to 7 cups unbleached all-purpose or high-gluten bread flour
⅓ cup nonfat dry milk or buttermilk powder
2 tablespoons unsalted butter, melted
1 tablespoon salt
Egg Yolk Glaze (page 118)
3 tablespoons poppy seeds

1 REPARING THE POTATO AND PROOFING THE YEAST: Peel the potato and cut into large pieces. Place in a 2-quart saucepan and cover with the water. Bring to a boil and cook until soft. Drain and reserve the liquid, adding more water as necessary to make 2 cups. Purée or mash the potato and set aside to cool. Warm or cool the potato water to 105° to 115°F and pour into a small bowl. Sprinkle the yeast and a pinch of the sugar over the potato water. Stir to combine and let stand until foamy, about 10 minutes.

2 MIXING THE DOUGH: In a large bowl using a whisk or in the bowl of a heavy-duty electric mixer fitted with a paddle attachment, combine 2 cups of the unbleached flour, the remaining sugar, the dry milk, butter, salt, mashed potatoes, and potato water. Beat hard until creamy, about 1 minute. Add the remaining flour, ½ cup at a time, until a soft, shaggy dough that just clears the sides of the bowl is formed. Switch to a wooden spoon when necessary if making by hand.

3 KNEADING: Turn the dough out onto a lightly floured work surface with the plastic pastry scraper and knead until soft and springy, 1 to 3 minutes for a machine-mixed dough and 4 to 7 minutes for a hand-mixed dough, dusting with flour only 1 tablespoon at a time, just enough as needed to prevent sticking. The dough will be smooth and springy. Do not let the dough get too dry by adding too much flour or the loaf will be very heavy.

4 FIRST RISE: Place the dough in a lightly greased deep container. Turn the dough once to coat the top and cover with plastic wrap. Let rise at room temperature until double in bulk, about 1 to 1½ hours.

5 SHAPING AND SECOND RISE: Turn the dough out onto a lightly floured work surface to deflate. Lightly grease the bottom and sides of the 9-by-5-inch loaf pans. Without working the dough further, divide it into 2 equal portions. Roll or pat each portion of dough into a rough rectangle and roll up each into a loaf shape. Place the loaves, seam side down, in the loaf pans. Cover loosely with plastic wrap and let rise at room temperature until the dough is fully double in bulk and about 1 inch over the rims of the pans, about 45 minutes.

6 BAKING OFF AND COOLING: Twenty minutes before baking, preheat the oven to 375°F. Brush the surfaces with egg glaze and sprinkle each loaf with half of the poppy seeds. Using a serrated knife, make 3 diagonal slashes across the top of the loaf, no more than ¼ inch deep. Place the pans on the center rack of the oven and bake for 40 to 45 minutes, or until the surface of the loaves is golden brown, the sides slightly contract from the pan, and the loaves sound hollow when tapped with your finger. Remove the loaves from the pans immediately to a cooling rack. Loaves are best slightly warm or at room temperature.

Potato Pan Rolls

Prepare the potato dough through Step 4 as directed and turn out onto a well-floured work surface. Pat the dough into a 12-by-18-inch rectangle about 1 inch thick. Dust the top of the dough with a good coating of flour. There will be flour on both the top and bottom surfaces. Using a downward motion, cut with a sharp knife into 4 sections on the short side and 6 sections on the long side, forming 24 pieces about 3 inches square. Place with the sides just touching in a large, greased open roasting pan or on a parchment-lined baking sheet or baking dish. Cover loosely with plastic wrap and let rise at room temperature for about 30 minutes. The rolls will be puffy and look like small cushions. Twenty minutes before baking, preheat the oven to 375°F. Bake the rolls in the center of the oven for 25 to 30 minutes, or until golden brown and firm to the touch. Serve warm, or cool on a rack.

Baker's Notes If you grow poppy flowers for seeds, order Hungarian blue bread seed poppies from Seeds of Change (1-505-438-8080). ◆ Poppy seeds tend to go rancid quickly, so store in the freezer along with your nuts and sesame seeds. ◆ Use a high-starch, floury baking potato for the best mashed potato breads rather than low-starch new potatoes, which contain more water.

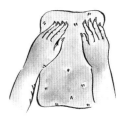

PATTING EACH PORTION INTO A RECTANGLE.

ROLLING UP EACH FROM THE LONG EDGE INTO A LOAF SHAPE.

PINCHING THE BOTTOM SEAL TO SEAM.

This is a bread with an attractive deep golden brown crust with a thick twist effect. The chewy texture is even throughout with a tight honeycombed crumb flecked with bran. It holds its shape when sliced, even when warm, and is excellent toasted.

Equipment

Small and large (at least 6-quart) mixing bowls
Measuring spoons and cups
Large balloon whisk and wooden spoon
Heavy-duty electric mixer with flat paddle attachment or dough hook (optional)
Plastic and metal dough scrapers
Dough container, preferably a 6-quart deep plastic container
Pastry brush
Cooling rack

Baking Pans and Yield

Two loaves using standard 9-by-5-inch metal, nonstick, glass, or clay loaf pans, greased on all inside surfaces, or 12 round buns or 16 long rolls using 2 greased or parchment-lined 11-by-16-inch baking sheets. If using glass or black-finish aluminum pans, reduce heat by 25°F.

Baking temperature
375°F

Timetable
Total preparation time About 3¼ hours
Working time 15 minutes
Kneading time About 5 minutes
First rise 1 to 1½ hours
Shaping time 5 to 10 minutes
Second rise 30 minutes

Perfect Whole Wheat Bread

The flavor of this whole wheat loaf is sweet, wholesome, and nutty. It was recommended to me by one of my baking students as a sure thing. A coarse grind of flour has lots of big bran and germ flecks, which make for a more crumbly loaf. It is important to retain the moisture in the dough by using plastic wrap during all risings; this prevents the formation of a crust, which would dry out the top of the loaf and prevent it from attaining a rounded dome during baking. This is a perfect beginning loaf utilizing whole wheat flour, as it uses only 40 percent whole wheat by volume paired with a high-protein white flour and an egg for extra leavening. The round and long rolls are great for burgers, hot dogs, and sandwiches.

BAKING TIME 35 TO 40 MINUTES FOR LOAVES, 18 TO 25 MINUTES FOR BUNS AND ROLLS

1 cup warm water (105° to 115°F)
2 tablespoons (2 packages) active dry yeast
Pinch of brown sugar
1 cup warm milk (105° to 115°F)
⅓ cup (packed) light brown sugar
3 tablespoons unsalted butter, melted
1 tablespoon salt
1 egg
2½ cups whole wheat flour, fine or medium grind
3½ to 4 cups unbleached all-purpose or high-gluten bread flour
Melted butter or olive oil for brushing

1 PROOFING THE YEAST: In a small bowl or 1-cup liquid measuring cup, pour ½ cup of the warm water. Sprinkle the yeast and the pinch of brown sugar over the surface of the water. Stir to dissolve and let stand at room temperature until foamy, about 10 minutes.

2 MIXING THE DOUGH: In a large bowl using a whisk or in the bowl of a heavy-duty electric mixer fitted with the paddle attachment, combine the remaining water, the milk, the ⅓ cup of brown sugar, melted butter, salt, egg, and the whole wheat flour. Beat hard until creamy, about 1 minute. Stir in the yeast mixture. Add the unbleached flour, ½ cup at a time, until a soft, shaggy dough that just clears the sides of the bowl is formed. Switch to a wooden spoon when necessary if making by hand.

3 KNEADING: Turn the dough out onto a lightly floured work surface with the plastic pastry scraper and knead until soft and springy, 1 to 3 minutes for a machine-mixed dough and 4 to 7 minutes for a hand-mixed dough, dusting with flour only 1 tablespoon at a time, just enough as needed to prevent sticking. The dough will be smooth and very springy with a slightly rough surface and sticky quality, but not dry. Do not add too much flour or the baked loaf will be dry and crumbly.

4 FIRST RISE: Place the dough in a lightly greased deep container. Turn the dough once to coat the top and cover with plastic wrap. Let rise at room temperature until double in bulk, about 1 to 1½ hours. Do not allow this bread to rise any higher than double, or it may collapse and bake into a flat loaf.

5 SHAPING AND SECOND RISE: Turn the dough out onto a lightly floured work surface to deflate. Lightly grease the bottom and sides of the 9-by-5-inch loaf pans. Clay pans are wonderful for this loaf. Divide the dough into into 4 equal portions. With the palms of your hands, roll into 4 fat sausages, each about 10 inches long. Place two of the pieces side by side. Starting in the center, wrap one around the other to create a fat twist effect. Repeat to form the second loaf. Place in the pans. Brush the tops with some of the melted butter or oil. Cover loosely with plastic wrap and let rise at room temperature until the dough is almost double in bulk and about 1 inch over the rims of the pans, about 30 minutes. These loaves need only a three-quarter proof for the best baked volume.

6 BAKING OFF AND COOLING: Twenty minutes before baking, preheat the oven to 375°F. Brush the tops with more butter or oil. Place the pans on the center rack of the oven and bake about 35 to 40 minutes, or until the surface of the loaves is golden brown, the sides slightly contract from the pan, and the loaves sound hollow when tapped with your finger. Remove the loaves from the pans immediately to a cooling rack. Loaves are best slightly warm or at room temperature.

Burger Buns

Grease or line 2 baking sheets with parchment. Turn the dough out onto the work surface and divide into 12 equal portions. Form each into a tight ball by rolling the dough with a cupped hand until smooth. Place, seam side down, at least 2 inches apart, on the baking sheet. Flatten each ball into a 1-inch-high disk with your palm. Use a second baking sheet rather than crowding the rolls. Cover loosely with plastic wrap and let rise in a warm place until puffy, about 20 minutes. Preheat the oven to 375°F. Bake in the center of the oven until slightly brown and firm to the touch, about 20 to 25 minutes. Place on a rack to cool before splitting.

Long Rolls

Grease or line 2 baking sheets with parchment. Turn the dough out onto the work surface and divide into 16 equal portions. Pat each portion into an oval and roll up from the long edge. Pinch the seams and round the ends to make an even cylinder, rather like a miniature French baguette. Place, seam side down, at least 1 inch apart, on the baking sheets. Flatten each cylinder slightly. Always use a second baking sheet rather than crowding the rolls. Cover loosely with plastic wrap and let rise in a warm place until puffy, about 20 minutes. Preheat the oven to 375°F. Bake in the center of the oven until slightly brown and firm to the touch, about 18 to 24 minutes. Place on a rack to cool before splitting.

Rosemary Whole Wheat Bread

Add 2 well-rounded teaspoons of well-crushed dried rosemary (or grind the herb in the food processor with ¼ cup of the whole wheat flour) to the dough in Step 2. Proceed to rise, shape, and bake as for Perfect Whole Wheat Bread.

Baker's Notes Whole wheat flour (ground from hard red winter wheat) contains gluten, but bread made from it rises more slowly and bakes up into a coarser textured loaf than that made with white flour because of the sharp-edged germ and bran, which cut the strands of gluten, especially during rising. Fine-grind flour with the germ and bran ground evenly into the flour bakes up into a finer textured bread than coarse-ground flour containing lots of bran and germ flecks. ◆ Whole wheat flour is compatible in flavor with glutenless specialty flours, such as buckwheat, brown rice, or barley. ◆ White whole wheat flour, ground from a strain of wheat with a white hull and a milder flavor, spelt flour, or graham flour can be substituted for regular whole wheat flour with excellent results. ◆ Perfect Whole Wheat Bread can be glazed with a Rich Egg Glaze (page 118) and sprinkled with sesame seeds or plain or honey-crunch wheat germ.

Storage
This bread has a good shelf life and does not stale quickly, staying moist for about 3 days. Store the unsliced bread or rolls wrapped in a plastic food storage bag at room temperature, or freeze (page 25).

Specific Skills
◆ Mixing and kneading a whole wheat straight dough.
◆ Shaping a two-strand twist.
◆ Shaping round and long buns.
◆ Rounding by hand.

Old-Fashioned Winter Oatmeal Bread

My friend of many years, Nancyjo Terres, gave me this excellent recipe, which was torn from an old calendar. She swore that it made the best oatmeal bread, hearty and soul satisfying. I agree. A cold climate grain, oats have a mildly sweet and nutty flavor. They are used in bread in Switzerland, Scandinavia, northern Europe, Ireland, and the British Isles. You may use rolled oats or quick-cooking flakes, which are smaller and absorb moisture quicker, interchangeably. Since oats have a low gluten content, they must be used with a high percentage of wheat flour to hold a loaf shape, otherwise the breads will be flat and very crumbly. Oat breads are highly nutritious, rich in minerals and protein.

BAKING TIME 40 TO 45 MINUTES

½ cup warm water (105° to 115°F)
1½ tablespoons (1½ packages) active dry yeast
Pinch of granulated sugar
2 cups warm milk (105° to 115°F)
½ cup honey
4 tablespoons (½ stick) unsalted butter, melted
1 tablespoon salt
2 cups rolled oats
5 to 5½ cups unbleached all-purpose or high-gluten bread flour
Extra rolled oats, for sprinkling
2 tablespoons melted unsalted butter, for brushing

1 PROOFING THE YEAST: In a small bowl or 1-cup liquid measuring cup, pour in the ½ cup of warm water. Sprinkle the yeast and sugar over the surface of the water. Stir to dissolve and let stand at room temperature until foamy, about 10 minutes.

2 MIXING THE DOUGH: In a large bowl using a whisk or in the bowl of a heavy-duty electric mixer fitted with the paddle attachment, combine the milk, honey, melted butter, salt, rolled oats, and 1½ cups of the unbleached flour. Beat hard until creamy, about 1 minute. Stir in the yeast mixture. Add the remaining flour, ½ cup at a time, until a soft, shaggy dough that just clears the sides of the bowl is formed. Switch to a wooden spoon when necessary if making by hand.

3 KNEADING: Turn the dough out onto a lightly floured work surface with the plastic pastry scraper and knead until soft and springy, 1 to 3 minutes for a machine-mixed dough and 4 to 7 minutes for a hand-mixed dough, dusting with flour only 1 tablespoon at a time, just enough as needed to prevent sticking. The dough will be smooth and springy with a nubby surface but not dry.

4 FIRST RISE: Place the dough in a lightly greased deep container. Turn the dough once to coat the top and cover with plastic wrap. Let rise at room temperature until double in bulk, about 1½ to 2 hours.

5 SHAPING AND SECOND RISE: Turn the dough out onto a lightly floured work surface to deflate. Grease the bottom and sides of the 8-by-4-inch loaf pans and sprinkle with rolled oats, or grease or line the baking sheet and sprinkle it with oats if making round loaves. Without working the dough further, divide it into 2 equal portions. Pat each portion of dough into a rough rectangle and roll each up into a loaf shape. Place the loaves, seam side down, in the pans. Or, form 2 round loaves. With your palms, press the portion gently to release trapped carbon dioxide and push the edges under to form a smooth top and rounded shape. Rotate the dough, pulling the top surface taut and tightly domed into the bottom center. Lift up the loaf and pull the bottom center together for extra tautness. This makes for a high, well-rounded baked loaf. If the loaf looks flat, repeat the process. Place the round loaves, seam-side down, on the baking sheet at least 4 inches apart to allow for expansion. Roll each loaf to attach some oats up the sides. Brush the tops with the melted butter. Cover loosely with plastic wrap and let rise at room temperature until the dough is fully double in bulk and about 1 inch over the rims of the pans, about 45 minutes.

6 BAKING OFF AND COOLING: Twenty minutes before baking, preheat the oven to 375°F. Brush the tops with the remaining melted butter and using a serrated knife, make 3 pairs of opposing diagonal slashes down the top of the loaf to form a herringbone V design, no more than ¼ inch deep. Place the pans on the center rack of the oven and bake about 40 to 45 minutes, or until the surface of the loaves is golden brown, the sides slightly contract from the pan, and the loaves sound hollow when tapped with your finger. Remove the loaves from the pans immediately to a cooling rack. Loaves are best slightly warm or at room temperature.

Baker's Notes Oat grains have no gluten. To avoid a flat loaf do not add more than about 1 cup oats to every 3 cups wheat flour to the dough. ♦ Some bakers presoak rolled oats, especially the sturdier regular or coarse Irish brands, in some of the liquid for about 1 hour to reduce moisture absorption during the rising periods. ♦ For a smoother texture, some bakers grind the oats to a coarse flour before making the dough. ♦ A good-quality granola cereal blend or mixture of rolled grains (such as rye, oats, and barley) can be substituted for the rolled oats. ♦ Maple syrup can be substituted for the honey for a distinctive and highly compatible flavor pairing with the oats.

Storage
Oatmeal breads have a good shelf life and do not stale quickly, staying moist about 3 days. Store the unsliced bread wrapped in a plastic food storage bag at room temperature, or freeze (page 25).

Specific Skills
♦ Preparing a straight dough with oats. ♦ Shaping a pan or round hearth loaf. ♦ Slashing a herringbone design.

Cornmeal Honey Bread

Cornmeal comes in several colors, from white to yellow to russet to blue, and a range of textures, from a coarse meal to a finely ground flour. It is a New World grain, part of the indigenous cuisines of the Americas. Distinctive bread recipes abound from the American Southwest natives, New Englanders, Southerners, Basque mountaineers, and northern Italians. Cornmeal should be used in small proportion to gluten-rich wheat flour. This extremely appetizing bread, which rises and bakes up like a fine-textured sandwich-type pan bread, is made with buttermilk. Originally the liquid strained after churning butter, thick tangy buttermilk is today made with special bacterial starters; it contributes to an especially tender crumb in yeast breads. Be prepared for the slightly coarse feeling texture of the dough during the kneading process.

BAKING TIME 40 TO 45 MINUTES

¾ cup warm water (105° to 115°F)

1 tablespoon (1 package) active dry yeast

Pinch of granulated sugar or 1 teaspoon honey

1½ cups warm buttermilk (105° to 115°F)

4 tablespoons (½ stick) unsalted butter, melted, or corn oil

⅓ cup honey, warmed slightly for easy pouring

1 tablespoon salt

1 cup yellow cornmeal, fine or medium grind

4½ to 5 cups unbleached all-purpose or high-gluten bread flour

Yellow cornmeal for sprinkling

2 tablespoons melted butter or corn oil, for brushing

1 PROOFING THE YEAST: In a small bowl or 1-cup liquid measuring cup, pour in the ¾ cup of warm water. Sprinkle the yeast and the sugar or honey over the surface of the water. Stir to dissolve and let stand at room temperature until foamy, about 10 minutes.

2 MIXING THE DOUGH: In a large bowl using a whisk or in the bowl of a heavy-duty electric mixer fitted with the paddle attachment, combine the buttermilk (do not worry if it has separated during heating), melted butter, honey, salt, cornmeal, and 1 cup of the unbleached flour. Beat hard until creamy, about 1 minute. Stir in the yeast mixture. Add the remaining flour, ½ cup at a time, until a soft, shaggy dough that just clears the sides of the bowl is formed. Switch to a wooden spoon when necessary if making by hand.

Appearance

This is a bread with a soft honeycombed texture and tight crumb, creamy-gold in color. It holds its shape when sliced, even when warm. It has a crisp, ruddy terracotta-hued thin crust over the entire loaf.

Equipment

Small and large (at least 6-quart) mixing bowls
Measuring spoons and cups
Large balloon whisk and wooden spoon
Heavy-duty electric mixer with flat paddle attachment or dough hook (optional)
Dough container, preferably a 6-quart deep plastic container
Plastic and metal dough scrapers
Serrated knife for scoring
Pastry brush
Cooling rack

Baking Pans and Yield

Two loaves using 8-by-4-inch metal, nonstick, glass, or clay loaf pans, greased on all inside surfaces, or 2 round loaves using 1 greased or parchment-lined 11-by-16-inch baking sheet. If using glass or black-finish aluminum pans, reduce heat by 25°F.

Baking Temperature

375°F

Timetable

Total preparation time About 4 hours
Working time 15 minutes
Kneading time About 5 minutes
First rise 1 to 1½ hours
Shaping time 5 to 10 minutes
Second rise About 45 minutes

Storage
Cornmeal breads have a good
shelf life and do not stale
quickly, staying moist about
3 days. Store the unsliced bread
wrapped in a plastic food
storage bag at room temperature,
or freeze (page 25).

Specific Skills:
• Integrating cornmeal into
a straight dough formula.
• Forming round hearth loaves.

SHAPING A
ROUND LOAF.

3 KNEADING: Turn the dough out onto a lightly floured work surface with the plastic pastry scraper and knead until soft and springy, 1 to 3 minutes for a machine-mixed dough and 4 to 7 minutes for a hand-mixed dough, dusting with flour only 1 tablespoon at a time, just enough as needed to prevent sticking. The dough will be smooth and springy with a close coarse surface but definitely not dry.

4 FIRST RISE: Place the dough into a lightly greased deep container. Turn the dough once to coat the top and cover with plastic wrap. Let rise at room temperature until double in bulk, about 1 to 1½ hours.

5 SHAPING AND SECOND RISE: Turn the dough out onto a lightly floured work surface to deflate. Grease the 8-by-4-inch loaf pans, or grease or line the baking sheet and sprinkle it with cornmeal if making round loaves. Without working the dough further, divide it into 2 equal portions. Pat each portion of dough into a rough rectangle and roll each up into a loaf shape. Place the loaves, seam side down, in the pans. Or, form 2 round loaves. Place the loaves, seam side down, on the baking sheet at least 4 inches apart to allow for expansion. Brush the tops with some of the melted butter or corn oil. Cover loosely with plastic wrap and let rise at room temperature until the dough is fully double in bulk and about 1 inch over the rims of the pans, about 45 minutes.

6 BAKING OFF AND COOLING: Twenty minutes before baking, preheat the oven to 375°F. Brush the tops with the remaining butter or corn oil and using a serrated knife, slash the loaves decoratively, no more than ¼ inch deep (I do 3 diagonals down the center for the pan loaves and a cross on the rounds). Place the pans on the center rack of the oven and bake for 40 to 45 minutes, or until the surface of the loaves is golden brown, the sides slightly contract from the pan, and the loaves sound hollow when tapped with your finger. Remove the loaves from the pans immediately to a cooling rack. Loaves are best slightly warm or at room temperature.

Baker's Notes Cornmeals come in a variety of grinds, from fine to coarse, with the main commercial meals made from yellow or white corn. Steel-ground degerminated cornmeal has had the germ and bran removed for longer shelf-life, but for the best flavor, search out fresh stone-ground meals, which retain them. • Store cornmeal in a tightly covered container in the refrigerator. Highly perishable stone-ground meals can be stored up to 4 months and degerminated meals up to 1 year. • Blue cornmeal, also known as Southwestern Hopi corn, is slightly grainier and sweeter than yellow corn; it makes a purple-pink to lavender to blue-green baked product depending on the type of ingredients it is combined with. It may be substituted for a similar grind of yellow or white meals. • Masa harina is whole hulled dried corn cooked and soaked in a lime-water bath, then ground. It is commonly used for making tortillas, but its unique taste is an excellent substitution in cornmeal bread doughs. • Cornmeal blends well with rye, whole wheat, and graham flours. It is a common addition to multi-grain breads. • The finer the grind, the more liquid it will absorb, producing a tighter-textured dough. Coarser grinds contain more surface husk, absorbing less. • Too much dusting during kneading and shaping makes for heavy streaks in the loaf. • Maple syrup can be substituted for the honey; it is an excellent flavor combination with cornmeal.

House French Bread

French bread in a variety of shapes and sizes is very popular in the United States as well as all over Europe, Africa, and South America. The bread is made from a simple lean dough with no added fat or sugar, and is referred to as a regular bread dough in France. They must be eaten within a few hours of baking or just warm for the best flavor and texture. Real crispy crusts are a result of sophisticated pressurized steam-injected ovens, which a home oven just cannot duplicate. A close approximation is to make your own simulated brick oven (page 30), but homebaked loaves will always have a side split from the expansion in a rather dry oven. Use a high-gluten bread flour for vigorous mixing, long, high rises, and good oven spring. Although semolina flour, sometimes called semolina pasta flour in the supermarket, is more often associated with Italian breads, it is a great high-gluten addition, as well as a subtle taste enhancer, to any lean white flour dough.

BAKING TIME 25 TO 30 MINUTES

2½ cups warm water (105° to 115°F)

1 tablespoon plus 1 teaspoon (1 package plus 1 teaspoon) active dry yeast

Pinch of granulated sugar

1 tablespoon granulated sugar, honey, barley malt syrup, or maple syrup

1 tablespoon salt

1½ cups semolina flour

5 to 5¼ cups unbleached high-gluten bread flour

Semolina flour, for dusting

1 egg white beaten with 1 tablespoon water for glaze

1 PROOFING THE YEAST: In a small bowl or 1-cup liquid measuring cup, pour in ½ cup of the warm water. Sprinkle the yeast and the pinch of sugar over the surface of the water. Stir to dissolve and let stand at room temperature until foamy, about 10 minutes.

2 MIXING THE DOUGH: In a large bowl using a whisk or in the bowl of a heavy-duty electric mixer fitted with the paddle attachment, combine the remaining water, sugar, salt, semolina flour, and 1 cup of the unbleached flour. Beat hard until creamy, about 1 minute. Stir in the yeast mixture. Add the remaining flour, ½ cup at a time, until a soft, shaggy dough that just clears the sides of the bowl is formed. Switch to a wooden spoon when necessary if making by hand.

3 KNEADING: Turn the dough out onto a lightly floured work surface with the plastic pastry scraper and knead until soft and springy, 1 to 3 minutes for a machine-mixed dough and 4 to 7 minutes for a hand-mixed dough, dusting with flour only 1 tablespoon at a time, just enough as needed to prevent sticking. The dough will be smooth and springy.

Appearance
This is a bread with an airy, open texture and creamy color. It holds its shape when sliced, even when warm. It has a thick tawny-brown crust that is hard and crisp directly after baking but that softens as it cools.

Equipment
Small and large (at least 6-quart) mixing bowls
Measuring spoons and cups
Large balloon whisk and wooden spoon
Heavy-duty electric mixer with flat paddle attachment or dough hook (optional)
Plastic and metal dough scrapers
Dough container, preferably a 6-quart deep plastic container
Pastry brush
Serrated knife for scoring
Spray pump water bottle
Cooling rack
Kitchen shears
Rolling pin

Baking Pans and Yields
Four baguettes using 2 greased or parchment-lined 11-by-16-inch baking sheets or two 17½-by-9-by-2½-inch perforated double-cradle nonstick baguette pans or black steel baguette pans.

Baking Temperature
425°F

Timetable
Total preparation time About 6½ hours
Working time 15 minutes
Kneading time About 5 minutes
First rise About 3 hours
Second rise About 2 hours
Shaping time 5 to 10 minutes
Final rise About 1 hour

4 FIRST AND SECOND RISES: Place the dough in a greased deep container. Sprinkle the top with flour and cover with plastic wrap. Let rise at room temperature until tripled in bulk, about 3 hours. Do not rush. Gently deflate the dough, transfer it to the work surface and knead about 6 to 8 times to release the trapped gases. Return the dough to the rising bucket. Let rise again until doubled in bulk, about 2 hours. This second rise is optional, but it makes for a more developed flavor and slightly better texture.

5 SHAPING AND FINAL RISE: Turn the dough out onto a lightly floured work surface to deflate. Grease or parchment-line the 2 baking sheets or baguette pans and dust with semolina flour. Without working the dough further, divide it into 4 even portions. Flatten each into a thin 14-by-6-inch rectangle with the palm of your hand. Starting at the long end, roll each up, using your thumbs to help roll tightly. With the side of your hand, define a depression lengthwise down the center of the dough. Fold over and pinch the seams to seal. Roll back and forth from the center out to form dough in a tight cylinder slightly shorter than your baking sheet or pan. Gently transfer, seam side down, to the prepared pans. Cover loosely with plastic wrap and let rise at room temperature until the dough is fully double in bulk, about 1 hour.

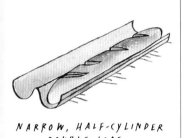

NARROW, HALF-CYLINDER
DOUBLE-LOAF
BAGUETTE PAN.

6 BAKING OFF AND COOLING: Twenty minutes before baking, preheat the oven to 425°F, and line with a baking stone or tiles, if desired. Brush the surfaces with egg glaze and with a serrated knife, slash 3 or 4 times on the diagonal, no more than ¼ inch deep. Just before placing in the oven, mist a few times with water from a clean spray pump bottle for moisture. Place the pans on the lowest rack of the oven. Three times, at 5-minute intervals after placing the loaves in the oven, open the oven door and spray the loaves quickly to create steam, taking care to protect your hands from burning. This step is totally optional. Do not pull the rack out of the oven. Bake for 25 to 30 minutes, or until the loaves are golden brown and sound hollow when tapped with your finger. Remove the loaves from the pans immediately to a cooling rack. Loaves are best slightly warm or at room temperature.

Bâtard

A *bâtard* is a large, oblong, torpedo-shaped loaf that looks like a short, fat baguette. Divide dough into 2 even portions. Pat each portion into a rectangle and tightly roll up, as for baguettes, but shape each roll into a 12-inch elongated oval with tapered ends and a thick middle section. Gently transfer, seam side down, to greased and dusted 15½-by-8-by-4-inch French bâtard cradle pans or a prepared baking sheet. With a serrated knife, slash the top 3 times on the diagonal, no deeper than ¼ inch, or make 1 long slash down the middle of each loaf. Glaze and bake as described in Step 6 for 35 to 40 minutes, or until the loaves are golden brown in color and sound hollow when tapped on the top and bottom with your finger. Remove the loaves from the pans immediately to a cooling rack.

Ficelle

This loaf is long, like a baguette, but only about 2 inches in diameter. Divide the dough into 6 even portions. Flatten each into a thin 14-by-6-inch rectangle with the palm of your hand. Form as for the baguettes. Gently transfer, seam side down, to the prepared baking sheets or baguette pans. Rise, glaze, and slash as for the baguettes in Step 6. Bake for about 20 minutes, or until the loaves are golden brown in color and sound hollow when tapped on the top and bottom with your finger. Remove the loaves from the pans immediately to a cooling rack.

Épi

This loaf is cut with kitchen shears to resemble a shaft of wheat. Cut the dough into 4 even portions and form each into a 12-inch baguette. Gently transfer, seam side down, to the prepared baking sheets. Holding kitchen shears at a 45° angle to the top surface and using quick motions with the shears (to prevent sticking and give a more earthy appearance), cut halfway into the dough. With your other hand, turn each piece to one side as it is cut. Cut at 3-inch intervals, turning each piece over the center to alternate sides, to resemble a head of wheat. You will have 6 to 8 cuts, depending on the size of the loaf. Let rise at room temperature only 25 minutes. Bake as described in Step 6 for 35 to 40 minutes, or until the loaves are golden brown in color and sound hollow when tapped with your finger. Remove the loaves from the pans immediately to a cooling rack. Take care with the épi after baking, as its sections can break apart easily.

Pain de Campagne

This is an oversized round country loaf. Roughly pat all of the dough into an thick, uneven circle. Pull up the sides and knead into the center of the loaf to create a tight round ball. Place, seam side down, on a prepared baking sheet. Let rise as in Step 5. Glaze and slash the top in a tic-tac-toe pattern. Bake as described in Step 6 for 45 to 50 minutes, or until the loaves are golden brown in color and sound hollow when tapped with your finger. Remove the loaves from the pans immediately to a cooling rack.

Boule

This is a small round country loaf. Divide dough into 4 equal portions. Form each into a tight round as for Pain de Campagne. Place, seam side down, on the prepared baking sheet. Let rise as in Step 5. Glaze and using a serrated knife or kitchen shears, slash an X on top, no deeper than ¼ inch. Bake as described in Step 6 for 25 to 30 minutes, or until the loaves are golden brown in color and sound hollow when tapped with your finger. Remove the loaves from the pans immediately to a cooling rack. Boules can also be shaped with a 3-strand braid layer (known as *la boule tressée*) or with 2 twisted strands to form a rope *(pain cordon)* or with a spiral *(pain spiral)* laid across the top after the final rise. These decorated loaves need no slashing.

Tricorne

This bread bakes into a rustic triangular loaf, similar to a 3-cornered hat or cushion. Divide the dough into 2 even portions on a lightly floured work surface. Form each portion into a ball and press to flatten into a thick disk. Measure the distance from the center of the disk to the edge with your thumb and index finger, noting the length (measuring the radius). With a rolling pin, roll out 3 equally spaced oval flaps, rolling out no more than 2 inches in from the edge of the dough, leaving a high rounded cushion of dough in the center. The flaps should be the same length as the one measured between your fingers (half the diameter of the round). Brush the surface of each flap with olive, walnut, or vegetable oil and fold it over into the center mound, with the flap ends just touching in the center. Place flap-side up on the prepared baking sheet. Dust with flour. Let rise as in Step 5. Glaze and bake as described in Step 6 for 30 to 35 minutes, or until the loaves are golden brown in color and sound hollow when tapped with your finger. The flaps will pop open during oven spring. Remove the loaves from the pans immediately to a cooling rack.

Champignon

A *Champignon* is a hearth loaf that is shaped like a rustic little mushroom. Divide the dough into 6 even portions. Further divide each piece into 2 uneven portions. Form the larger piece into a tight round. Form the smaller piece into a round and place on top of the larger ball. With a floured finger, poke a hole in the center of the stacked rounds to make them adhere to each other. Place, topknot up, on the prepared baking sheet. Rise only 15 to 20 minutes, as the mushroom shape becomes less defined the longer it rises. Gently redefine the hole to keep the topknot intact, although it may tip to one side or the other after baking. Glaze and bake as described in Step 6 for 20 to 25 minutes, or until the loaves are golden brown in color and sound hollow when tapped on with your finger. Remove the loaves from the pans immediately to a cooling rack.

Petits Pains

These are crusty little French rolls. Divide the dough into 20 equal portions. Form each into a small round or oval. With rounds, form into tight balls as for miniature *boules.* With ovals, pinch ends to form a spindle shape, a thick middle with tapered ends. Using a serrated knife, slash the tops of the rounds with a cross and the ovals once down middle, no deeper than ¼ inch. Place, seam side down, on the prepared baking sheets. Let rise only 15 minutes, at room temperature. Glaze and bake as described in Step 6 for 15 to 20 minutes, or until the loaves are golden brown in color and sound hollow when tapped with your finger. Remove the loaves from the pans immediately to a cooling rack.

Fougasse

Fougasse is a flatbread made in the south of France. The dough can be left plain or embellished by the addition of 1 cup chopped sundried tomatoes with 2 tablespoons of their oil; chopped fresh herbs; or whole or halved pitted olives during the mixing in Step 2. Divide the dough into 2 portions. Dust the bench with flour to keep the dough from sticking. With a rolling pin, roll the dough into a large irregular oval shape, about 1 inch thick. If the dough becomes resistant, let it rest on the bench for 5 minutes to relax before proceeding. Using a sharp paring knife or kitchen shears, cut about six 4-inch sliver cuts at irregular intervals or pairs of diagonal cuts, all the way through the dough, to create an open lattice-work flatbread or rustic treelike shape. The other classic shape looks like an over-sized madeleine tea cake or baseball glove. For that shape, roll each portion of the dough into a thick 8-by-10-inch rectangle. Lay your outstretched hand on the dough and cut 4 slits all the way through the dough, using your fingers as a guide. Leave the dough connected at all sides. Let rise about 15 minutes and bake as described in Step 6 for 15 to 20 minutes, or until the loaves are golden brown in color. Serve immediately, breaking apart with your hands to eat.

Onion Rolls

FLATTENING THE ROLLS.

> 1 recipe House French Bread dough
> 4 tablespoons unsalted butter
> 2 large yellow onions, coarsely chopped
> ¼ cup heavy cream
> Cornmeal or semolina for sprinkling

PREPARING THE ONION MIXTURE: While the dough is rising, melt butter in a large heavy skillet over medium heat and sauté the onions until just soft but not browned, stirring frequently, about 15 minutes. Add the cream, increase the heat to high, and reduce the liquid by half. The mixture will be very thick. Set aside to cool to room temperature.

SHAPING AND BAKING OFF THE ROLLS: Preheat the oven to 425°F. Turn the dough out onto the work surface and divide into 16 equal portions. Form each into a round ball. Place about 2 inches apart on 2 greased or parchment-lined baking sheets sprinkled with cornmeal or semolina. Using kitchen shears or a sharp knife, snip a ½-inch-deep X into the center of each roll. With your fingers, press a deep depression in the center of each X. Place 1 to 2 tablespoons of onion mixture into the center depression of each roll. Place the rolls immediately on the lowest rack of the oven. Bake for 15 to 18 minutes, or until golden brown and crusty.

Baker's Notes Use a good-quality water in your baking, such as bottled spring water. Soft water, such as distilled water, or hard tap water, which is possibly chlorinated, should be avoided. ◆ If you are using a baking peel and baker's tiles rather than a baking sheet, make certain there is a thick coating of cornmeal or semolina on the wooden peel to prevent sticking and facilitate easy shoveling onto the hot tiles in the oven. ◆ These breads are baked in a hot oven, but not as hot as for pizza, as they would not bake evenly. ◆ Baguette pans are 2 half-cylinders joined at one side or with braces that mold the loaves into long rods. The pans come in thin or thick widths; the perforated pans enable the heat to bake all sides of the loaf, making the bottom crust crispy as well. ◆ Baguettes and *ficelles* end up with approximately a 50-50 ratio of crust to soft interior crumb. Larger loaves will have more crumb in proportion to crust. ◆ Be certain to get the pale cream-yellow semolina flour, rather than the coarsely ground meal similar in texture to farina and used as a substitute for coarse cornmeals. ◆ An equal amount of regular whole wheat, spelt, or kamut flour may be substituted for the semolina flour.

Storage
House French Bread loaves and rolls are made from a lean dough and begin to stale immediately after they cool. They are best eaten within a few hours of baking spread with butter or dipped in olive oil. Eat the rolls and *Fougasse* directly out of the oven! Store the unsliced bread or rolls wrapped in a plastic food storage bag at room temperature, or freeze (page 25). Day-old Onion Rolls are excellent split, spread with butter, and grilled on the cut side only in a frying pan until crisp. The day-old bread is great for croutons or slices of toast to float in soups.

Specific Skills
Preparing a classic lean straight dough. ◆ Forming classic country bread shapes. ◆ Lean dough fermentation. ◆ High temperature baking.

Country Bread
with Walnuts and Raisins

Here is a country-style peasant loaf that has a crisp crust and soft interior. It utilizes the same straight dough technique as the French bread, but also combines three kinds of flour with bran and is embellished with golden raisins and walnuts for strong body and natural sweetness. The bread rises easily but will not have as open a texture as long-rise or sponge-starter breads. Still, the flavor is rich and extremely aromatic. Serve warm with cheeses.

BAKING TIME 45 TO 50 MINUTES

2½ cups warm water (105° to 115°F)

1½ tablespoons (1½ packages) active dry yeast

Pinch of granulated sugar

2 tablespoons walnut oil

1 tablespoon salt

¼ cup unprocessed bran

¾ cup medium-grind rye flour

¾ cup whole wheat flour

½ cup dark or golden raisins

½ cup coarsely chopped walnuts

4 to 4½ cups unbleached all-purpose or high-gluten bread flour

Yellow cornmeal or farina, for dusting

1 PROOFING THE YEAST: In a small bowl or 1-cup liquid measuring cup, pour in ¾ cup of the warm water. Sprinkle the yeast and the sugar over the surface of the water. Stir to dissolve and let stand at room temperature until foamy, about 10 minutes.

2 MIXING THE DOUGH: In a large bowl using a whisk or in the bowl of a heavy-duty electric mixer fitted with the paddle attachment, combine the remaining water, the oil, salt, bran, rye flour, and whole wheat flour. Beat hard until creamy, about 1 minute. Stir in the yeast mixture and 1 cup of the unbleached flour. Beat 30 seconds. Add the raisins and nuts. Add the remaining unbleached flour, ½ cup at a time, until a soft, shaggy dough that just clears the sides of the bowl is formed. Switch to a wooden spoon when necessary if making by hand.

Storage
Country Bread with Walnuts and Golden Raisins has a good shelf life and does not stale quickly, staying moist about 3 days. Store the unsliced bread wrapped in a plastic food storage bag at room temperature, or freeze (page 25).

Specific Skills
Preparing a straight dough with embellishments. ♦ Shaping a round hearth loaf.

3 KNEADING: Turn the dough out onto a lightly floured work surface with the plastic pastry scraper and knead until soft and springy, 1 to 3 minutes for a machine-mixed dough and 4 to 7 minutes for a hand-mixed dough, dusting with flour only 1 tablespoon at a time, just enough as needed to prevent sticking. The dough will be smooth and springy with a slight tacky texture.

4 FIRST RISE: Place the dough in a lightly greased deep container. Turn the dough once to coat the top and cover with plastic wrap. Let rise at room temperature until double in bulk, about 1½ to 2 hours.

5 SHAPING AND SECOND RISE: Turn the dough out onto a lightly floured work surface to deflate. Grease or line the baking sheet and sprinkle it with cornmeal or farina. Form the dough into a large round loaf as described on page 66. Lift up the loaf and pull the bottom center together for extra tautness. This makes for a high, well-rounded baked loaf. Roll the surface of the loaf in flour to coat. Place, seam side down, on the baking sheet. Cover loosely with plastic wrap and let rise at room temperature until the dough is fully double in bulk, about 1 hour.

6 BAKING OFF AND COOLING: Twenty minutes before baking, preheat the oven to 400°F, with a baking stone or tiles, if desired. With a serrated knife, slash the loaf decoratively with a single line across the center to give the effect of dividing the loaf in two, or with 4 lines to create a square, no more than ¼ inch deep. Place the baking sheet on the center rack of the oven and bake for 45 to 50 minutes, or until the surface is golden brown and the loaf sounds hollow when tapped with your finger. Transfer the loaf immediately to a cooling rack. The loaf is best slightly warm or at room temperature.

Baker's Notes This bread may also be baked in the La Cloche clay baker (page 31). ♦ Different grinds of whole wheat flour will affect the finished texture of the loaf slighty. Graham or spelt flours may be substituted. ♦ This loaf may be made with lightly toasted walnuts.

Italian Whole Wheat Bread

Lean Italian breads are very similar in appearance to French and country breads. A moderate percentage (25 percent by volume) of whole wheat flour contributes to the flavor, color, and texture of the bread. It has short fermentation times and introduces you to a sponge starter. This bakes up into a light textured bread with a crisp crust. The kaiser rolls are large, crusty sandwich buns made from the same dough, but shaped into a five-sided pinwheel.

BAKING TIME 35 TO 40 MINUTES FOR ROUNDS, 25 TO 30 MINUTES FOR BAGUETTES,
18 TO 22 MINUTES FOR ROLLS

Sponge

1 tablespoon (1 package) active dry yeast

Pinch of granulated sugar

1¾ cups tepid water (100°F)

1 cup whole wheat flour

1½ cups unbleached all-purpose or high-gluten bread flour

Dough

2½ teaspoons salt

1½ to 1¾ cups unbleached all-purpose or high-gluten bread flour

Cornmeal or coarse semolina, for dusting

1 PREPARING THE SPONGE: Sprinkle the yeast and sugar over the tepid water in a medium (3- or 4-quart) bowl or plastic container and stir until dissolved. Let stand until foamy, about 10 minutes. Add the whole wheat flour and the unbleached flour. With a whisk, beat hard until smooth. Cover loosely with plastic wrap and let stand at room temperature 4 hours. This sponge can be stored overnight or for 1 week in the refrigerator before using.

2 MIXING THE DOUGH: Add the salt and ½ cup of the flour to the sponge. Beat hard with a whisk for 10 minutes, or for 5 minutes in a heavy-duty electric mixer fitted with the paddle attachment. With a wooden spoon, add the remaining flour as needed to make a soft dough.

3 KNEADING: Turn the dough out onto a lightly floured surface and knead vigorously to create a soft, moist, elastic dough that will still feel sticky, 5 to 7 minutes, adding flour only 1 tablespoon at a time as needed. Use a dough scraper to clean off the film of dough that accumulates on the work surface as you go along. Take care not to add too much flour; this dough should just hold its shape yet retain a definitely moist, tacky quality.

Appearance
This is a bread with an airy, open texture with a deep creamy interior that is lightly flecked with russet bran. It holds its shape when sliced, even when warm. It has a tawny-brown crust that is crisp directly after baking but that softens as the bread cools.

Equipment
Small and large (at least 6-quart) mixing bowls
Measuring spoons and cups
Large balloon whisk and wooden spoon
Heavy-duty electric mixer with flat paddle attachment or dough hook (optional)
Dough container, preferably a 6-quart deep plastic container
Plastic and metal dough scrapers
Baking stone
Serrated knife for scoring
Cooling rack

Baking Pans and Yield
One large round hearth loaf, 2 medium long loaves, or 8 kaiser rolls using 1 greased or parchment-lined 11-by-16-inch baking sheet or 1 perforated double-cradle baguette pan or black steel baguette pan.

Baking Temperature
425°F

Timetable
Total preparation time About 6½ hours
Sponge fermentation time 4 hours
Working time 15 minutes
Kneading time 5 to 7 minutes
Bench rest 20 minutes
Shaping time 5 to 10 minutes
Rising time 1 to 1½ hours

Storage

Italian Whole Wheat Bread and Kaiser Rolls are made from a lean dough and begin to stale immediately after they cool. They are best eaten within a few hours of baking, but will keep 2 days. Store the unsliced bread wrapped in a plastic food storage bag at room temperature, or freeze (page 25). This bread makes great croutons.

Specific Skills

Preparing a short sponge starter and mixing the dough.
• Working with whole wheat flour. • Working with a bench rest. • Shaping cylindrical loaves and kaiser rolls.

4 BENCH REST AND SHAPING: Cover the dough with a clean dish towel and let it rest 20 minutes. Grease or parchment-line the baking sheet or grease the baguette form pan and dust with cornmeal or semolina. Shape dough into 1 large round loaf or divide into 2 equal portions and form into baguettes. Transfer to the baking sheet or baguette pan. Cover loosely with plastic wrap and let rise at room temperature until tripled in volume, about 1 to 1½ hours.

5 BAKING OFF AND COOLING: Twenty minutes before baking, preheat the oven to 450°F, with a baking stone or tiles placed on the lowest rack. If using a peel, slide shaped and risen loaves gently onto a baker's paddle heavily sprinkled with cornmeal or semolina; otherwise leave undisturbed. Using a serrated knife, gently slash the top of loaves with a cross for the round hearth loaf and diagonal slashes for the long loaves, no deeper than ¼ inch. Slide in the oven onto the hot stone, or place the baking sheet or baguette pan directly on the hot stone in the preheated oven. Immediately reduce the oven temperature to 425°F and bake the round loaf for 35 to 40 minutes and the baguettes for 25 to 30 minutes, or until the surface of the loaves is golden brown and they sound hollow when tapped with your finger. Remove the loaves from the pans immediately to a cooling rack. Loaves are best slightly warm or at room temperature. Cut with a knife or break with the hands into pieces.

Whole Wheat Kaiser Rolls

Shaping the rolls by hand: Turn the dough out onto the work surface and divide into 8 equal portions. Using your palm or a rolling pin, flatten each portion into a 1-inch-thick round disk about 7 inches in diameter. If the dough is hard to roll out, let it rest for 5 minutes. Fold a small flap portion (about one-fifth of the dough) from the outer edge into the center. Rotate around the edge, turning up side flaps to make 5 slightly overlapping folds, with the last fold covering the remaining space and the edge of the first fold. It should look like a pinwheel. Press into the center with your fingers to seal the pattern.

Grease or parchment-line the baking sheet and sprinkle it with poppy seeds or dust with flour. Place the rolls, pattern side down to retain the definition, at least 2 inches apart on the prepared baking sheet. Dust the bottoms with cornmeal or semolina. Use a second baking sheet rather than crowding the rolls. Cover loosely with plastic wrap and let rise in a warm place until puffy, about 30 minutes. Preheat the oven to 375°F. Using a plastic spatula, gently turn the rolls right side up, taking care not to deflate them. Bake in the center of the oven until lightly browned and firm to the touch, about 18 to 22 minutes. Cool on a rack before splitting.

Shaping the rolls with a kaiser roll cutter: Form each portion into a tight ball. Flatten each portion into a 5-inch disk with your palm. Let rest 15 minutes, covered with a clean, damp dish towel. Stamp each roll firmly with a 2½-inch kaiser roll cutter, pressing halfway into the dough for the pinwheel pattern definition. Do not cut all the way through. Rise and bake off the same way as for hand-shaped rolls.

Baker's Notes The crust is not very dark brown due to the whole wheat flour and lack of sugar. • Barley malt powder or syrup may be used to feed the sponge in place of the sugar.

Cottage Cheese Dill Bread

Cottage Cheese Dill Bread is totally addictive upon first bite. Once exclusive to rural and mountain farms, fresh curd cheese is slightly acid, like buttermilk, and often is added to old-fashioned country breads. This fresh soft cheese contributes its unique ultra-moist texture and savory herbal fragrance that borders on a perfume. Make a round or pan loaf for sandwiches and toast, or a long baguette for thin-sliced cocktail sandwiches.

BAKING TIME 45 TO 55 MINUTES

1¼ cups warm water (105° to 115°F)

1 tablespoon (1 package) active dry yeast

3 tablespoons granulated sugar or honey

5 to 5½ cups all-purpose or high-gluten bread flour

2 small shallots, minced

¼ cup vegetable or olive oil

¼ cup chopped fresh dill or 3 tablespoons dried dillweed

1 tablespoon salt

2 eggs

1 cup small-curd cottage cheese

Egg Yolk Glaze (page 118)

1 PREPARING THE SPONGE AND THE SHALLOTS: In a medium bowl or deep plastic container, pour in the warm water. Sprinkle the yeast and the sugar over the surface of the water. Stir to dissolve and add 2 cups of the flour. Beat hard with a whisk until creamy and well combined, about 15 strokes. Cover loosely with plastic wrap and let stand at room temperature until bubbly, about 1 hour. Meanwhile, prepare the shallots. In a small skillet, sauté the shallots in the oil until translucent. Set aside to cool to room temperature.

2 MIXING THE DOUGH: In a large bowl using a whisk or in the bowl of a heavy-duty electric mixer fitted with the paddle attachment, pour the sponge and 1 cup of the flour, the dill, salt, eggs, cottage cheese, and cooled shallots with all of their oil. Beat hard until creamy, about 1 minute. Add the remaining flour, ½ cup at a time, until a soft, shaggy dough that just clears the sides of the bowl is formed. Switch to a wooden spoon when necessary if making by hand.

Appearance
A fluffy freeform or pan loaf with a cream-colored interior flecked with green, high-volume, and close, very moist grain. The soft thin crust is deep golden brown and sometimes topped with a shiny wash.

Equipment
Medium and large (at least 6-quart) mixing bowls
Small skillet
Measuring spoons and cups
Large balloon whisk and wooden spoon
Heavy-duty electric mixer with flat paddle attachment or dough hook (optional)
Plastic and metal dough scrapers
Dough container, preferably a 6-quart deep plastic container
Pastry brush
Serrated knife for scoring
Cooling rack

Baking Pans and Yield
Two round or long loaves using a greased or parchment-lined 11-by-16-inch baking sheet or 2 pan loaves using 8-by-4-inch metal, nonstick, glass, or clay loaf pans, greased on all inside surfaces. If using glass or black-finish aluminum pans, reduce the heat by 25°F.

Baking Temperature
350°F

Timetable
Total preparation time About 4¼ hours
Sponge fermentation time 1 hour
Working time 15 minutes
Kneading time About 5 minutes
First rise 1 to 1¼ hours
Shaping time 5 to 10 minutes
Second rise 30 minutes

3 KNEADING: Turn the dough out onto a lightly floured work surface with the plastic pastry scraper and knead until soft and springy, 1 to 3 minutes for a machine-mixed dough and 4 to 7 minutes for a hand-mixed dough, dusting with flour only 1 tablespoon at a time, just enough as needed to prevent sticking. The dough will be delicate, smooth, and lightly springy to the touch, not dry yet able to hold its shape.

4 FIRST RISE: Place the dough in a lightly greased deep container. Turn the dough once to coat the top and cover with plastic wrap. Let rise at room temperature until just double in bulk, about 1 to 1¼ hours. Do not let the dough rise more than double at this point or it will collapse in the oven.

5 SHAPING AND SECOND RISE: Turn the dough out onto a lightly floured work surface to deflate. Grease or parchment-line the baking sheet or grease the 8-by-4-inch loaf pans. Without working the dough further, divide it into 2 equal portions. Roll or pat each portion of dough into a round. Or form each portion into a rough rectangle and roll it up into a standard loaf shape. Place the loaves, seam side down, in the pans. Cover loosely with plastic wrap and let rise at room temperature until the dough is almost double in bulk and 1 inch over the rims of the pans, about 30 minutes. It is important that this loaf gets no more than a three-quarter proof.

6 BAKING OFF AND COOLING: Twenty minutes before baking, preheat the oven to 350°F. Brush the surfaces with the egg glaze and using a serrated knife, slash the loaves decoratively (I do 3 diagonals for the rectangular loaves and a cross on the rounds), no more than ¼ inch deep. Place the pans on the center rack of the preheated oven and bake for 45 to 55 minutes, or until the surface of the loaves are golden brown, and the sides slightly contract from the pan and sound hollow when tapped with your finger. These loaves will rise a lot in the oven. Remove the loaves from the pans immediately to a cooling rack. Do not slice until thoroughly cooled. Loaves are best served at room temperature.

Baker's Notes If using dried dillweed, make sure it is fresh and aromatic. ♦ This bread makes outrageous croutons. ♦ Pay particular attention to the rising times. This is a delicate dough that can collapse easily during oven spring if overrisen. ♦ This loaf may also be made with ricotta cheese, German-style quark, or fresh goat cheese to vary the texture and flavor slightly.

Country-style Whole Wheat Pita

The simplest and most basic of all yeast breads to make, pita, also known as Middle Eastern pocket bread, is a small round of dough about the size of a tortilla that puffs dramatically when baked in a hot oven on a baking sheet or unglazed hot stone. Pitas are an ancient daily bread, often baked on a grill over an open fire, around the Mediterranean. They are often patted out into large rounds that extend to the baker's elbow. While they puff in the oven, they collapse as they cool, with a pocket inside that is perfect for filling.

BAKING TIME 8 TO 10 MINUTES

2½ cups warm water (105° to 115°F)

1 tablespoon (1 package) active dry yeast

Pinch of granulated sugar

¼ cup olive oil

1 tablespoon salt

3 cups whole wheat pastry flour

3 to 3½ cups unbleached all-purpose flour

1 PROOFING THE YEAST: In a small bowl or 1-cup liquid measuring cup, pour in ½ cup of the water. Sprinkle the yeast and the pinch of sugar over the surface of the water. Stir to dissolve and let stand at room temperature until foamy, about 10 minutes.

2 MIXING THE DOUGH: In a large bowl using a whisk or in the bowl of a heavy-duty electric mixer fitted with the paddle attachment, combine the remaining water, olive oil, salt, and whole wheat pastry flour. Beat hard until creamy, about 1 minute. Stir in the yeast mixture. Add the unbleached flour, ½ cup at a time, until a soft, shaggy dough that just clears the sides of the bowl is formed. Switch to a wooden spoon when necessary if making by hand.

3 KNEADING: Turn the dough out onto a lightly floured work surface with the plastic pastry scraper and knead until soft and springy, 1 to 2 minutes for a machine-mixed dough and 3 to 5 minutes for a hand-mixed dough, dusting with flour only 1 tablespoon at a time, just enough as needed to prevent sticking. Leave the dough moist and soft yet at the same time smooth and springy.

4 FIRST RISE: Place the dough in a lightly greased deep container. Turn the dough once to coat the top and cover with plastic wrap. Let rise at room temperature until double in bulk, about 1 to 1½ hours.

Appearance

Soft, flat rounds of light brown bread with no crust. The dry outer surface and the small amount of inner crumb are the same color; the texture is slightly airy. Pita tend to be doughy if eaten hot, soft and chewy when cooled.

Equipment

Small and large (at least 6-quart) mixing bowls
Measuring spoons and cups
Large balloon whisk and wooden spoon
Heavy-duty electric mixer with flat paddle attachment or dough hook (optional)
Plastic and metal dough scrapers
Dough container, preferably a 6-quart deep plastic container
Rolling pin
Wide metal spatula
Cooling rack

Baking Pans and Yield

Sixteen 6-inch round flatbreads using 2 ungreased or parchment-lined 11-by-16-inch baking sheets and/or baking stone and peel.

Baking Temperature

475°F

Timetable

Total preparation time: About 3 hours
Working time 15 minutes
Kneading time About 5 minutes
First rise 1 to 1½ hours
Shaping time 20 to 25 minutes
Second rise 15 minutes

Storage

Pitas should be eaten as soon as they are cool the day they are baked or wrapped in a clean kitchen towel to keep warm until serving. Store in plastic bags at room temperature for 1 day, or freeze (page 25).

Specific Skills

Attention to fermentation periods. ◆ Shaping dough with a rolling pin. ◆ Placing and baking flatbreads on heated baking stone.

ROLLING OUT
THE DOUGH BALLS.

WARM FROM
THE OVEN.

5 SHAPING AND SECOND RISE: Preheat the oven to 475°F, with a baking stone set on the bottom rack, if desired. Line several baking sheets; it is not necessary to grease them. Or, heavily flour a peel. Gently deflate the dough and divide it in half. Cover 1 half with plastic wrap or a clean towel to prevent forming a skin. Divide into 8 equal portions and form each into a ball. Let rest 10 minutes while dividing the second section of dough. Dust the work surface with whole wheat pastry flour. Using a rolling pin, roll the balls into 6-inch circles about ¼-inch thick. Loosely cover the circles on the bench. Do not stack, as they would stick together. If the dough does not roll out easily, let it rest for 10 minutes to relax the gluten. Move the dough circles by draping them one at a time over a flour-dusted rolling pin to place them on a floured kitchen towel before transferring to the peel or baking sheets. Let rest 15 minutes, until puffy.

6 BAKING OFF AND COOLING: Transfer the circles to a peel or baking sheet. With a quick action of the wrist, slide the pita rounds from the peel directly onto the hot stone. Four will fit at once. Or place the baking sheets, one at a time, on the bottom rack directly on the hot stone, if using. Do not open the oven door for a full 4 minutes, as the puff begins almost immediately. Bake 8 to 10 minutes, until fully puffed and light brown. Watch carefully that the pitas do not overbake or burn. The baking sheet pitas will take longer to bake than the stone-baked ones. Remove the puffed hot breads with a wide metal spatula to stack between clean kitchen towels.

Baker's Notes It is important to roll out the dough evenly. If the circles are too thick, the pita will not puff; if they're too thin, you will have crackers; if they're uneven, only sections will puff. ◆ Wear heavy oven mitts to protect your hands when transferring the pitas. ◆ For an all white flour pita, substitute unbleached all-purpose flour for the whole wheat pastry flour. Do not use bread flour, as the pita may be too tough. ◆ One-third cup of a specialty flour, such as soy, barley, chestnut, or brown rice flour, may be substituted for an equal amount of whole wheat pastry flour. ◆ For sesame pitas, sprinkle sesame seeds on the work surface and roll the dough ball into them, coating all surfaces, before rolling out the pita.

My Favorite Buttermilk Dinner Rolls

Dinner rolls are made from a rich soft roll dough which is easy to sculpt into a variety of shapes. It contains more sugar and fat than that for lean hard rolls, like French Petits Pains or Kaiser Rolls. Dinner rolls are well suited to freezing at several steps during the formation of the dough and they hold up nicely for up to twenty-four hours of retarded rising in the refrigerator before baking. Buttermilk creates an exceptionally tender product.

BAKING TIME 15 TO 18 MINUTES

1 tablespoon (1 package) active dry yeast

Pinch of granulated sugar

¼ cup warm water (105° to 115°F)

1 cup warm buttermilk (105° to 115°F)

2 tablespoons granulated sugar or honey

Grated zest of 1 lemon

¼ cup (½ stick) unsalted butter, melted, or olive oil

1 egg

2 teaspoons salt

4 to 4½ cups unbleached all-purpose flour

Egg Yolk Glaze (page 118)

3 tablespoons sesame, poppy, or fennel seeds

1 PROOFING THE YEAST: Combine the yeast, sugar, and warm water in a small bowl and stir to dissolve. Let stand until foamy, about 10 minutes.

2 MIXING THE DOUGH: In a large bowl using a whisk or in the bowl of a heavy-duty electric mixer fitted with the paddle attachment, combine the buttermilk, sugar, zest, melted butter, egg, and salt. Stir in 1½ cups of the flour and beat hard for 2 minutes, or until the mixture is smooth and creamy. Add flour ½ cup at a time with a wooden spoon until a soft dough that just clears the sides of the bowl is formed. Switch to a wooden spoon when necessary if making by hand.

3 KNEADING AND FIRST RISE: Turn the dough out onto a lightly floured surface and knead until soft, smooth, and elastic, 1 to 3 minutes for a machine-mixed dough and 4 to 7 minutes for a hand-mixed dough, dusting with flour only 1 tablespoon at a time, just enough as needed to prevent sticking. Place in a greased bowl, turn once to grease the top, and cover with plastic wrap. Let rise at room temperature until double in bulk, about 1 to 1½ hours.

Appearance

Individual soft rolls in different sizes and shapes with a cream-colored interior, high volume, and close grain. The pliant hairline-thin crust is deep golden brown; it can be topped with a shiny wash and/or seeds.

Equipment

Small and large (at least 6-quart) mixing bowls
Measuring spoons and cups
Large balloon whisk and wooden spoon
Heavy-duty electric mixer with flat paddle attachment or dough hook (optional)
Plastic and metal dough scrapers
Dough container, preferably a 6-quart deep plastic container
Rolling pin
Pastry brush
Chef's knife or pastry wheel
Serrated knife or kitchen shears for scoring
Cooling rack

Baking Pans and Yield

Sixteen dinner rolls using 2 greased or parchment-lined 11-by-16-inch baking sheets.

Baking temperature:

375°F

Timetable

Total preparation time About 3 hours
Working time 15 minutes
Kneading time About 5 minutes
First rise 1 to 1½ hours
Shaping time 10 minutes
Second rise 30 minutes

4 SHAPING AND SECOND RISE: Turn the dough out onto a lightly floured surface. Grease or parchment-line the 2 baking sheets. Divide the dough in half, then roll each half into a 2- to 3-inch cylinder. With the metal dough scraper or chef's knife, cut the cylinder into 8 equal portions. Repeat with the second cylinder, making a total of 16 equal portions. Shape each piece of dough into a small oval. Cover loosely with plastic wrap and let rise at room temperature until double in bulk, about 30 minutes. Soft rolls are given a full proof.

5 BAKING OFF AND COOLING: Twenty minutes before baking, preheat the oven to 375°F. Gently brush each roll with egg glaze and sprinkle with seeds, if desired, or leave plain. Using a serrated knife or kitchen shears, gently cut 2 or 3 diagonal slashes no more than ¼ inch deep on the top surface of each roll. Place in the center of the oven and bake for 15 to 18 minutes, or until golden brown. If using 2 baking sheets, place on the upper and lower racks, and switch positions halfway through baking. Remove from pans and cool on a rack. Serve warm, or cool to room temperature and reheat. Unless otherwise specified, this baking method applies to all the shapes below.

Bow Knots and Rosettes

Cut the dough in half and then divide each portion into 8 equal portions. Roll each piece into a 10-inch rope ½ inch in diameter. To make a Bow Knot, tie loosely in a knot, leaving 2 long ends. For a Rosette, tuck one end over and under the roll; bring the other end up and over to tuck into the roll center. Place the rolls about 2 inches apart on the prepared baking sheet.

BOW KNOT

Braided Rolls

Divide the dough into 3 equal portions. Roll each portion into a rope about 24 inches long. Place the ropes side by side and braid them loosely. Cut the braid into 16 equal portions and pinch the ends to taper them.

BRAID

Butterfly Rolls

Roll the dough into a 10-by-20-inch rectangle. Brush the surface with melted butter. Roll up, from the long edge, jelly-roll fashion. Place seam side down and, with the metal bench scraper or chef's knife, cut the log into 18 equal portions. Press each portion in the center with the handle of a wooden spoon laid across the top to create a fan effect out of the sides.

BUTTERFLY

CLOVERLEAF

CRESCENT

PARKER HOUSE

SNAIL

Cloverleaf Rolls

Divide the dough in half, then each half into 8 equal portions. Pinch off 3 equal pieces of the dough from each portion (a total of 48 pieces) and shape each into 1-inch smooth balls. Place 3 balls touching each other in each of 16 greased standard muffin cups.

Crescent Rolls

Cut the dough in half. On a lightly floured work surface, roll each half into an 8-inch circle. Brush with corn oil. With a knife or pastry wheel, cut each circle into 8 equal wedges. Beginning at the wide end, firmly roll each wedge up toward the point. Place, point side down, on the prepared baking sheets and curve the ends inward.

Double Crescent Rolls

Cut the dough in half. Roll each piece into a 10-by-6-inch rectangle about ¼ to ½ inch thick. Cut each into 3 long strips. Roll each strip into a 10-inch rope. Divide each rope into 3 equal pieces. Roll each piece and taper the ends. Shape into a half-circle. Lay 2 crescents back to back on the prepared baking sheets. The crescents should be just touching. Lay a small strip of dough over the center and tuck it underneath on each side.

Parker House

Turn the dough out onto the lightly floured work surface and roll out into a 12-inch square about ½ to ¾ inch thick. Using a sharp knife or pastry wheel, cut the dough into 4 equal sections across and 4 lengthwise to form sixteen 3-inch squares. Stretch each one slightly to elongate it and, using the handle of a wooden spoon to mark the fold, mark the roll lengthwise a little off center. Fold the small half over the larger half. Press the folded edge gently to adhere. Place 1 inch apart on baking sheets.

Snails

Cut the dough in half and divide it into 8 equal portions. Roll each portion into an 8-inch-long rope ½ inch in diameter. Starting at one end, wind the strip of dough around itself to form a spiral. Tuck the edge firmly underneath.

Refrigerator Rolls

METHOD ONE: After kneading the dough in Step 3, place it in a greased deep container, bowl, or gallon-size plastic food storage bag. Brush the surface of the dough with melted butter or oil. Cover tightly with plastic wrap or seal the bag, leaving room for the dough to expand. Refrigerate for up to 4 days, deflating the dough as necessary.

To form refrigerator rolls, remove the amount of dough desired about 3 hours before serving. Shape as desired. Place on greased or parchment-lined baking sheets, cover loosely with plastic wrap, and let rise at room temperature until almost double, about 1½ to 2 hours. Bake as directed in Step 5.

METHOD TWO: After the dough has risen in Step 3, gently deflate it and shape the rolls. Place on parchment-lined baking sheets and brush the tops with melted butter. Cover loosely with oiled wax paper or parchment, then with plastic wrap, taking care to cover all edges tightly. Immediately refrigerate for 2 to 24 hours.

When ready to bake off refrigerator rolls, remove the pans from the refrigerator, uncover, and let stand at room temperature for 20 to 30 minutes while preheating the oven. Bake as directed in Step 5.

Freezer Rolls

Mix, rise, and shape the rolls as directed in Steps 1 through 4. Place on a nonstick, disposable, or parchment-lined baking sheet that will fit into your freezer. Cover tightly with plastic wrap. Freeze until firm, about 2 to 3 hours. Remove the rolls from the baking sheet and transfer to a plastic freezer bag. Freeze the rolls for up to 2 weeks but no longer, as the leavening power of the yeast will begin to decrease.

To defrost and serve freezer rolls, unwrap the frozen rolls and place on a greased or parchment-lined baking sheet. Cover loosely with plastic wrap and let stand at warm room temperature to rise until double in bulk, 4 to 6 hours. The dough may also be thawed out overnight in the refrigerator. Bake as directed in Step 5.

Homemade Brown-and-Serve Rolls

Mix, rise, and shape the rolls as directed in Steps 1 through 4. Place on greased or parchment-lined sheets, cover loosely with plastic wrap, and let rise at room temperature until doubled in bulk, 1½ to 2 hours. Ungreased disposable aluminum baking pans are perfect. Bake in the center of a preheated 300°F oven until the rolls are fully baked, but not browned, 15 to 20 minutes. Remove from the pan and cool on a rack. Place the rolls in a heavy-duty plastic bag and refrigerate for up to 3 days or freeze for up to 3 weeks.

To serve, let the frozen rolls thaw at room temperature in the bag. Place in a single layer on an ungreased or parchment-lined baking sheet. Bake in a preheated 375°F oven until golden brown, 10 to 15 minutes.

Baker's Notes If your rolls bake up pale and sour, the dough may be overfermented. ◆ If your rolls bake up very moist, the dough may be underfermented. ◆ If rolls bake up flat, check your mixing method and rising times. Perhaps too much flour was added during kneading. ◆ The rolls may be brushed with melted butter before and just after baking for an ultra-soft crust.

Storage
Homemade rolls are best eaten within a few hours of baking. Store the rolls in a plastic food storage bag at room temperature, or freeze (page 25).

Specific Skills
◆ Preparing a classic soft roll dough. ◆ Shaping small strands of dough into knots, snails, etc. ◆ Proofing rolls. ◆ Introduction to retarded refrigerator dough and freezing techniques.

Pumpernickel Raisin Bread

This is an eastern European dark bread known as chornyi khleb *in Russian. It is a sweet rye bread, in comparison to sour starter ryes, and utilizes the straight-dough method to make a soft oblong loaf. It has coffee, molasses, raisins, and cocoa added to darken and sweeten the dough in place of traditional caramel coloring and toasted bread crumbs. The flour is a medium grind of rye, which makes for a higher loaf with a finer and moister texture than heavy dark rye flour. Bran and whole wheat flour are added for a more complicated dimension to the taste. This bread is best at room temperature, even better the next day. It is great with creamy cheese spreads and for sandwiches; it is also excellent toasted and spread with butter and honey.*

BAKING TIME 35 TO 40 MINUTES

2¼ cups warm water (105° to 115°F)

2 tablespoons (2 packages) active dry yeast

Pinch of granulated sugar or 1 teaspoon molasses

4 tablespoons (½ stick) unsalted butter, melted

⅓ cup light or dark molasses

1½ tablespoons instant espresso powder

1 tablespoon salt

1 tablespoon caraway seeds

1 teaspoon fennel seeds

¼ cup unsweetened cocoa powder or carob powder

½ cup whole wheat flour

½ cup unprocessed bran

2 cups medium-grind rye flour

3 to 3½ cups unbleached all-purpose or high-gluten bread flour

¼ cup yellow cornmeal

¼ cup sesame seeds

1 tablespoon whole wheat flour

2 cups dark raisins, soaked in hot water and drained on paper towels

Egg Yolk Glaze (page 118)

1 PROOFING THE YEAST: In a small bowl or 1-cup liquid measure, pour in ¾ cup of the warm water. Sprinkle the yeast and sugar over the surface of the water. Stir to dissolve and let stand at room temperature until foamy, about 10 minutes.

Appearance
This is a bread with a firm, even, honeycombed texture flecked with bran and seeds. The tight crumb is very dark brown in color. It holds its shape when sliced and softens considerably when cooled. The smooth dark umber-brown crust is the same color as the interior. The flavor is sweet and hearty.

Equipment
Small and large (at least 6-quart) mixing bowls
Measuring spoons and cups
Large balloon whisk and wooden spoon
Heavy-duty electric mixer with flat paddle attachment or dough hook (optional)
Plastic and metal dough scrapers
Dough container, preferably a 6-quart deep plastic container
Rolling pin
Pastry brush
Baking stone (optional)
Serrated knife for scoring
Cooling rack

Baking Pans and Yield
Two large oblong loaves using 1 greased or parchment-lined 11-by-16-inch baking sheet.

Baking Temperature
375°F

Timetable
Total preparation time About 3½ hours
Working time 15 minutes
Kneading time About 5 minutes
First rise 1 to 1½ hours
Shaping time 5 to 10 minutes
Second rise 45 minutes

2 MIXING THE DOUGH: In a large bowl using a whisk or in the bowl of a heavy-duty electric mixer fitted with the paddle attachment, combine the remaining water, melted butter, molasses, espresso powder, salt, caraway and fennel seeds, cocoa, whole wheat flour, bran, and rye flour. Beat until creamy, about 1½ minutes. Stir in yeast mixture and beat 1 minute more. Add the unbleached flour, ½ cup at a time, until a soft, shaggy dough that just clears the sides of the bowl is formed. Switch to a wooden spoon if making by hand. This dough will be sticky.

3 KNEADING: Turn the dough out onto a lightly floured work surface with the plastic pastry scraper and knead until soft and springy, 1 to 3 minutes for a machine-mixed dough and 4 to 7 minutes for a hand-mixed dough, dusting with flour only 1 tablespoon at a time, just enough as needed to prevent sticking. The dough will be smooth and springy with a tacky quality. Do not add too much flour or the loaves will be dry and dense.

4 FIRST RISE: Place the dough in a lightly greased deep container. Turn the dough once to coat the top and cover with plastic wrap. Let rise at room temperature until double in bulk, about 1 to 1½ hours.

5 SHAPING AND SECOND RISE: In a small bowl, combine the cornmeal, 1 tablespoon of the sesame seeds, and 1 tablespoon whole wheat flour. Grease or parchment-line a baking sheet and sprinkle with the mixture. Turn the dough out onto a lightly floured work surface to deflate. Without working the dough further, divide it into 2 equal portions. Roll or pat each portion into a rough rectangle about 10-by-12 inches. Sprinkle each rectangle evenly with 1 cup of the raisins and roll up tightly. The loaf will be about 10 inches long. Place the loaves, seam side down, on the baking sheet, coating the bottoms well with the cornmeal-sesame mixture. Cover loosely with plastic wrap and let rise at room temperature until fully double in bulk, about 45 minutes.

6 BAKING OFF AND COOLING: Twenty minutes before baking, preheat the oven to 375°F, with a baking stone placed on the middle rack, if possible. Brush the surface and exposed sides of both loaves with the egg glaze and sprinkle heavily with sesame seeds. With a serrated knife, slash the loaves decoratively with 4 diagonals, no more than ¼ inch deep. Place the pans on the center rack of the oven and bake about 35 to 40 minutes, or until the surface of the loaves is chocolate brown and the loaves sound hollow when tapped with your finger. Take care not to overbake, as the center should remain moist. Remove the loaves from the pans immediately to a cooling rack.

Baker's Notes Rye doughs are most often baked hearth style. ◆ Rye breads are best with strong flavor enhancers, such as sour starters, molasses, dark brown sugar, fennel, orange, onions, and caraway. ◆ Rye breads vary in color according to the type of rye flour used. ◆ The denser the rye bread, the lower the oven temperature for even baking. ◆ The gluten content of rye flour is low (2 percent), and it is not the same type of gluten as in wheat flour. Consequently, rye doughs can easily rise sideways instead of straight up. ◆ Medium rye flour contains about 12 percent protein, as compared to dark rye flour, which contains 14 to 16 percent protein.

Storage
Rye breads with butter, molasses, and chocolate have a good shelf life and do not stale quickly, staying moist about 3 days. Store the unsliced bread wrapped in a plastic food storage bag at room temperature, or freeze (page 25).

Specific Skills
◆ Mixing a straight dough with mixed flours, brans, dried fruit, and whole grains. ◆ Forming a freestanding loaf. ◆ Observation of fermentation periods.

Country White Hearth Bread

This is a classic rustic European-style bread made with a sponge. Note that the technique varies from the direct method recipes in that it calls for cool liquids, a small amount of yeast, an initial rising with a sponge, long rises, and a high baking temperature. A semiliquid sponge, or preliminary culture, allows for an initial period of fermentation that begins to develop the gluten and gives the bread a fine texture and flavorful tang similar to a mellow sourdough. Any salt and fat required by the recipe are added with the remaining ingredients in the later stages when the dough is formed. Although the dough takes two days to make, do not be put off. The dough is mixed, risen, formed, and baked as for any other bread recipe. It is easy to handle and the resulting bread is of superior quality. It is baked into one large round loaf on a hot baking stone. Please try all the variations to this recipe; whole-grain flours are added in small amounts to the basic dough, changing the texture and flavor dramatically.

BAKING TIME 40 TO 45 MINUTES

Sponge

1 teaspoon active dry yeast

⅓ cup warm water (90° to 100°F)

⅔ cup milk, at room temperature

1 teaspoon honey, maple syrup, or barley malt syrup

2 cups unbleached all-purpose flour

Dough

1 teaspoon active dry yeast

2 cups water, at room temperature

¼ cup good quality olive oil

1 tablespoon salt

About 4¾ to 5½ cups unbleached all-purpose flour

1 PREPARING THE SPONGE: In a large bowl or deep plastic container, sprinkle the yeast over warm water and milk. Stir to dissolve. Add the honey and flour. Beat with a whisk until smooth. Cover loosely with plastic wrap and let stand at room temperature for about 4 hours. It will be bubbly. This sponge can be stored overnight or up to 1 week in the refrigerator before using, if necessary.

2 MIXING THE DOUGH: In a large bowl using a whisk or in the bowl of a heavy-duty electric mixer fitted with the paddle attachment, carefully add the yeast, water, olive oil, salt, 1 cup of the flour, and the sponge; the mixture will be soupy at first. Beat hard with the whisk for 3 minutes, or for 1 minute in the mixer on medium speed after the sponge is incorporated into the water. Add the remaining flour ½ cup at a time, switching to a wooden

Appearance
This recipe makes a bread with a strong grain-sweet flavor combined with a hint of sour from the starter and a moist, airy interior full of irregular holes. The golden brown crust is thick and highly domed. The loaves are soft yet easy to slice and have a rich, robust aroma and distinctive whole-grain character.

Equipment
Small and large (at least 6-quart) mixing bowls
Measuring spoons and cups
Large balloon whisk and wooden spoon
Heavy-duty electric mixer with flat paddle attachment or dough hook (optional)
Plastic and metal dough scrapers
Dough container, preferably a 6-quart deep plastic container
Serrated knife for scoring
Wire cooling rack

Baking Pans and Yield
One large or 2 small loaves using 1 parchment-lined 11-by-16-inch baking sheet.

Baking Temperature
400°F

Timetable
Total preparation time About 9½ to 28 hours
Sponge fermentation time 4 hours
Working time 10 minutes
Kneading time 5 to 8 minutes
First rise 3 to 12 hours
Shaping time 5 to 10 minutes
Second rise 1 to 3 hours

SCROLL

CROSS

HERRINGBONE

DIAMOND

LEAF CUT

spoon when necessary if making by hand. The dough will be smooth, yet sticky enough not to pull away from the sides of the bowl.

3 KNEADING: Turn the dough out onto a lightly floured surface and knead vigorously until very elastic, yet still moist and tacky, 1 to 3 minutes for a machine-mixed dough and 4 to 7 minutes for a hand-mixed dough, dusting with flour only 1 tablespoon at a time, just enough as needed to prevent sticking. This is important for a good, light texture. Slam the dough hard against the work surface to develop the gluten. Set aside, uncovered, for 5 to 10 minutes. Knead again, and the sticky dough will smooth out without any extra flour.

4 FIRST RISE: Place in an ungreased deep container and keep covered with plastic wrap to prevent the surface from drying. Let rise at room temperature until triple in volume, 3 hours to overnight.

5 SHAPING AND SECOND RISE: Remove the dough from the container. Place on the lightly floured work surface and flatten slightly to deflate. Divide the dough in half for two loaves or leave intact for one. With the smooth surface facing up, push the rounded sides of the dough underneath toward the center with your fingers and outside of the hands. It is easy to rotate the dough at this point and pull at the center to make a tight dome that holds its own shape. If the loaf is not taut enough, repeat this procedure. Dust the top lightly with more flour and place in a dusted cloth-lined basket *(banneton)* or on a flour-dusted or parchment-lined baking sheet, smooth side down. Let rise, uncovered, at room temperature until soft, springy, and double to triple in bulk, 1 to 3 hours.

6 BAKING OFF AND COOLING: Twenty minutes before baking, preheat the oven to 400°F with a baking stone, if desired. Turn the loaf or loaves out of the *bannetons,* if using, onto a well-floured peel, or leave the risen loaf on the baking sheet. Using a serrated knife, slash a criss-cross design into the top of the loaves, no deeper than ¼ inch. Immediately slide the baking sheet into the hot oven (or carefully invert the loaves directly onto the baking stone from the *bannetons*) and bake until very dark and crusty, about 40 to 45 minutes (do not worry if the one large loaf takes up to 55 minutes). Remove from the pan to cool on a rack.

Country Cornmeal Hearth Bread

In Step 2, substitute 1½ cups medium-grind yellow cornmeal for an equal amount of unbleached flour. The total amount of unbleached flour used will be about 3½ cups.

Country Wheat and Barley Hearth Bread

In Step 2, substitute 1¼ cups stone-ground whole wheat flour and ⅓ cup barley flour for an equal amount of unbleached flour. The total amount of unbleached flour used will be about 4 cups.

Country Wheat and Rye Hearth Bread

In Step 2, substitute ½ cup each coarse stone-ground whole wheat flour and coarse rye meal (also known as pumpernickel flour) for an equal amount of unbleached flour. The total amount of unbleached flour used will be about 4 cups.

Country White Hearth Bread with Bran

In Step 2, substitute 1⅓ cups unprocessed wheat, rice, or oat bran for ¾ cup unbleached flour during the mixing. The total amount of unbleached flour used will be about 4 cups.

Country White Hearth Bread with Olives

In Step 2, substitute ½ cup stone-ground or white whole wheat flour and ½ cup medium rye flour for an equal amount of unbleached flour. Then incorporate 1½ cups of pitted large black olives toward the end of the kneading. It is okay if the olives break up during the working. The total amount of unbleached flour used will be 3½ to 4 cups.

Country White Hearth Bread with Raisins

In Step 5, flatten the dough into a thick rectangle. Plump 2½ cups dark raisins in hot water for 10 minutes; drain and dry on paper towels. Sprinkle the raisins over the dough, kneading lightly to distribute evenly.

Baker's Notes The fermentation time of the sponge depends on the quality of flour, the type of yeast, and the humidity. ◆ This is the oldest known method for fermenting European-style doughs. Breads made with a yeast-fortified sponge starter appeared in Europe after the discovery of cultured yeasts in the mid-seventeenth century.

Storage
Country White Hearth Bread and its variations have a good shelf life due to the fermented starter, staying moist about 3 days and not staling quickly. Store wrapped in a plastic food storage bag at room temperature, or freeze (page 25).

Specific Skills
• Preparing a sponge and mixing a sponge-type dough. • Blending flours, brans, and cracked grains. • Forming a hearth loaf. • Attention to fermentation periods. • Using a baking stone and peel.

Swedish Rye Bread

This rye bread dough looks as if it will be dense and hard to work. On the contrary. Although the gluten in rye is different from the gluten in wheat—an all-rye loaf will be very dense—the even combination of the two flours makes for a soft, workable dough that rises high and is elastic to work with. This is a sweet rye bread in the Scandinavian tradition, with the traditional flavoring of molasses, orange, and spicy seeds; the straight-dough method is best here, as rye flour does not need long mixing.

BAKING TIME 25 TO 30 MINUTES

1¾ cups warm water (105° to 115°F)

1 tablespoon (1 package) active dry yeast

Pinch of light brown sugar

¼ cup light or dark unsulfured molasses

¼ cup (packed) light or dark brown sugar

2 tablespoons unsalted butter, melted, or vegetable oil

1 tablespoon salt

2 teaspoons caraway or fennel seeds

Grated zest of 1 large orange or lemon

2½ cups medium-grind rye flour

2¼ to 2½ cups unbleached all-purpose or high-gluten bread flour

Melted butter, for brushing (optional)

1 PROOFING THE YEAST: In a small bowl or 1-cup liquid measuring cup, pour in ¾ cup of the warm water. Sprinkle the yeast and the sugar or honey over the surface of the water. Stir to dissolve and let stand at room temperature until foamy, about 10 minutes.

2 MIXING THE DOUGH: In a large bowl using a whisk or in the bowl of a heavy-duty electric mixer fitted with the paddle attachment, combine the remaining water, molasses, brown sugar, melted butter or oil, salt, seeds, zest, and rye flour. Beat hard until creamy, about 1 minute. Stir in the yeast mixture. Add the unbleached flour, ½ cup at a time, until a soft, shaggy dough that just clears the sides of the bowl is formed. Switch to a wooden spoon when necessary if making by hand.

3 KNEADING: Turn the dough out onto a lightly floured work surface with the plastic pastry scraper and knead until soft and springy, 1 to 3 minutes for a machine-mixed dough and 4 to 7 minutes for a hand-mixed dough, dusting with flour only 1 tablespoon at a time, just enough as needed to prevent sticking. The dough will be smooth and springy with a definite tacky quality. It is very important that this dough not be too dry.

Appearance

This is a compact, slightly flat peasant-style loaf with a tight, coarse texture and a smooth, very deep brown crust from the molasses. The oval loaves are soft yet easy to slice and have a rich, robust aroma and distinctive slightly sour, whole-grain character.

Equipment

Small and large (at least 6-quart) mixing bowls
Measuring spoons and cups
Large balloon whisk and wooden spoon
Heavy-duty electric mixer with flat paddle attachment or dough hook (optional)
Plastic and metal dough scrapers
Dough container, preferably a 6-quart deep plastic container
Serrated knife for scoring
Pastry brush
Cooling rack

Baking Pans and Yield

Two oval loaves using 1 greased or parchment-lined 11-by-16-inch baking sheet.

Baking Temperature

375°F

Timetable

Total preparation time About 5 hours
Working time 15 minutes
Kneading time About 5 minutes
First rise 2 to 2½ hours
Shaping time 5 to 10 minutes
Second rise 2 hours

PULLING THE
BOTTOM OF THE LOAF
TOGETHER.

4 FIRST RISE: Place the dough in a lightly greased deep container. Turn the dough once to coat the top and cover with plastic wrap. Let rise at room temperature until double in bulk, about 2 to 2½ hours. Do not let rise more than double or the dough will overferment.

5 SHAPING AND SECOND RISE: Turn the dough out onto a lightly floured work surface to deflate. Grease or parchment-line the baking sheet. Without working the dough further, divide the dough into 2 equal portions. Form into two oval balls. Lift up the loaf and pull the bottom center together for extra tautness. This makes for a high, well-rounded baked loaf. If the loaf is flat, repeat the process. Place the loaves, seam side down, on the baking sheet. Brush the tops with the melted butter or dust with flour, as desired. Cover loosely with plastic wrap and let rise at room temperature until the dough is fully double in bulk, about 2 hours.

6 BAKING OFF AND COOLING: Twenty minutes before baking, preheat the oven to 375°F. Using a serrated knife, slash the loaves decoratively with 3 diagonals, no more than ¼ inch deep. Place the pan on the center rack of the oven and bake about 25 to 30 minutes, or until the loaves are golden brown and sound hollow when tapped with your finger. Remove the loaves from the pans immediately to a cooling rack. Loaves are best slightly warm or at room temperature.

Baker's Notes I like the combinations of lemon with fennel seeds and orange with caraway. ◆ Rye doughs bake best in a moderate oven. Expect this sweet rye to get its crust color very quickly. ◆ Since rye flour cannot rise as high as wheat flours, do not let the dough rise over double in bulk, otherwise the gluten strands will break and the dough will deflate. It is also important not to overrise rye doughs, as they may collapse in the oven. ◆ Rye doughs will burst open on the sides during oven spring if the dough has not been risen long enough or if the crust forms too rapidly in an overly hot oven. ◆ The darker, or coarser, the grind of rye and the more bran and germ is left in, the denser your bread will be. ◆ Rye flour is a good flavor match with oats, buckwheat, barley, and wild rice.

Harvest Bread

Harvest bread is full of cracked whole grains, specialty flours, and whole bran. I use a seven-grain cereal mixture available in health food stores for an easy combination of rye, oats, wheat, barley, millet, flax, and corn grits. The dough is most efficiently mixed slowly in an electric mixer, but it also makes up beautifully by hand. The loaves also have only a three-quarter proof so as not to tear and rupture the delicate gluten, causing a collapse during glazing and slashing. This is a recipe that demands a light hand, lots of observation, and timing judgement to create a moist whole grain loaf.

BAKING TIME 40 TO 45 MINUTES

1½ cups boiling water

1 cup 7-grain cereal

1 cup rolled oats

4 tablespoons (½ stick) unsalted butter, cut into pieces, or sunflower seed oil

¾ cup honey

1 cup warm water (105° to 115°F)

2 tablespoons (2 packages) active dry yeast

Pinch of granulated sugar or 1 teaspoon honey

1 cup warm milk (105° to 115°F)

1 tablespoon salt

⅓ cup sesame seeds

½ cup unprocessed bran

½ cup medium-grind rye flour

1 cup whole wheat flour

4¾ to 5¼ cups unbleached all-purpose or high-gluten bread flour

Polenta or other coarsely ground cornmeal, for sprinkling

3 tablespoons melted butter or oil, for brushing

1 PRESOAKING THE CEREAL: In a medium bowl, pour the boiling water over the cereal and rolled oats. Add the butter and honey. Let stand at room temperature for 1 hour.

2 PROOFING THE YEAST: In a small bowl or 1-cup liquid measure, pour in ¾ cup of the warm water. Sprinkle the yeast and sugar over the surface of the water. Stir to dissolve and let stand at room temperature until foamy, about 10 minutes.

Appearance

A bread with a firm texture with an even distribution of cracked grains and grits. The coarse, dense crumb is light brown in color. It holds its shape when sliced. Harvest Bread has a crusty russet-brown crust. The flavor is distinctive and hearty.

Equipment

Small, medium, and large (at least 6-quart) mixing bowls
Measuring spoons and cups
Large balloon whisk and wooden spoon
Heavy-duty electric mixer with flat paddle attachment or dough hook (optional)
Plastic and metal dough scrapers
Dough container, preferably a 6-quart deep plastic container
Pastry brush
Baking stone (optional)
Serrated knife for scoring
Cooling rack

Baking Pans and Yield

Three medium round loaves using 1 greased or parchment-lined 11-by-16-inch baking sheet.

Baking Temperature

375°F

Timetable

Total preparation time About 5½ hours
Presoak 1 hour
Working time 15 minutes
Kneading time About 5 minutes
First rise 1½ to 2 hours
Shaping time 5 to 10 minutes
Second rise 1 hour

3 MIXING THE DOUGH: In a large bowl using a whisk or in the bowl of a heavy-duty electric mixer fitted with the paddle attachment, combine the remaining water, the milk, salt, sesame seeds, bran, rye flour, and whole wheat flour. Beat hard until creamy, about 1 minute. Stir in the yeast mixture and soaked grains. Beat 1 minute more. Add the unbleached flour, ½ cup at a time, until a soft, shaggy dough that just clears the sides of the bowl is formed. Switch to a wooden spoon when necessary if making by hand. This dough will be sticky.

4 KNEADING: Turn the dough out onto a lightly floured work surface with the plastic pastry scraper and knead until soft and springy, 1 to 3 minutes for a machine-mixed dough and 4 to 7 minutes for a hand-mixed dough, dusting with flour only 1 tablespoon at a time, just enough as needed to prevent sticking. The dough will be smooth and very springy with a tacky, nubby quality. Do not add too much flour or loaves will be dry and dense.

5 FIRST RISE: Place the dough in a lightly greased deep container. Turn the dough once to coat the top and cover with plastic wrap. Let rise at room temperature until double in bulk, about 1½ to 2 hours. The dough will spring back lightly when touched gently. Do not overrise or the dough may collapse from the weight of the grains.

6 SHAPING AND SECOND RISE: Turn the dough out onto a lightly floured work surface to deflate. Grease or parchment-line a baking sheet and sprinkle with polenta. Without working the dough further, divide it into 3 equal portions. Form each portion into a tight round. Place the loaves, seam side down, on the baking sheet. Brush the tops with melted butter or oil to prevent drying. Cover loosely with plastic wrap and let rise at room temperature until the dough is just double in bulk, about 1 hour. Heavy whole grain breads get only a three-quarter proof.

7 BAKING OFF AND COOLING: Twenty minutes before baking, preheat the oven to 375°F, with a baking stone placed on the middle rack, if possible. With a serrated knife, slash the loaves decoratively with a cross, no more than ¼ inch deep. Place the baking sheet on the center rack of the oven and bake for 40 to 45 minutes, or until the loaves are deep brown and sound hollow when tapped with your finger. Take care not to overbake. Remove the loaves immediately to a cooling rack and brush the tops with melted butter, if desired.

Baker's Notes If bread is very crumbly, it is because there was too high a percentage of whole grains and too much flour added during kneading. ◆ It is essential that the whole grains receive a short presoak to allow for more efficient moisture absorption. Unsoaked grains result in a very stiff dough. ◆ Poppy seeds can be substituted for half of the amount of sesame seeds for a flavorful variation.

Storage
Whole-grain breads with milk and honey have a good shelf life and do not stale quickly, staying moist about 2 days, but this loaf is best the day it is baked. Store the unsliced bread wrapped in a plastic food storage bag at room temperature, or freeze (page 25). Makes great toast!

Specific Skills
◆ Presoaking grains. ◆ Mixing a straight dough with a heavier percentage of cracked and rolled whole grains and a variety of flours. ◆ Attention to kneading and dough consistency. ◆ Observation of fermentation periods.

Hungarian Sweet Cheese Bread

This recipe became a standard in my teaching repertoire and was consistently voted the favorite sweet bread. Do not worry about the shaping technique; the dough is pliable and easy handled. Sour cream is a common feature in European sweet doughs; its acidity and richness lend a unique tangy flavor and smooth texture.

BAKING TIME 35 TO 40 MINUTES

Dough

1½ tablespoons (1½ packages) active dry yeast

Pinch of granulated sugar

½ cup warm water (105° to 115°F)

1 cup (2 sticks) unsalted butter, at room temperature

½ cup granulated sugar

4 large eggs

1 cup (8 ounces) sour cream

1 teaspoon salt

Grated zest of 1 lemon

5½ to 6 cups unbleached all-purpose flour

Melted butter, for greasing pans

Hungarian Pastry Cheese

8 ounces natural cream cheese, at room temperature

8 ounces fresh goat cheese, at room temperature

1 cup granulated sugar or vanilla sugar (page 34)

4 large eggs

1 tablespoon fresh lemon juice

Apricot Brandy Glaze

¾ cup good quality apricot jam, puréed in a blender or food processor until smooth

3 tablespoons brandy, Cognac, or orange liqueur

1 PROOFING THE YEAST: In a small bowl, sprinkle the yeast and sugar over the warm water. Stir to dissolve and let stand until foamy, about 10 minutes.

Appearance

The fluted tube pans make an attractive wreath shape. The center hollow can be filled with flowers or fresh fruit. The crumb is creamy in color with an even distribution of air pockets encasing a dense sweet cheese filling. The thin crust is dark brown.

Equipment

Small, medium, and large (at least 6-quart) mixing bowls

Measuring spoons and cups

Large balloon whisk and wooden spoon

Heavy-duty electric mixer with flat paddle attachment or dough hook (optional)

Plastic and metal dough scrapers

Dough container, preferably a 6-quart deep plastic container

Pastry brushes

Rolling pin

Kitchen shears

Plastic or metal spatula for spreading

Cooling rack

Food processor or blender

Small saucepan

Baking Pans and Yield

Two small bundt cakes using two 6-cup fluted mini bundt pans. If the pans are black-finished, reduce the heat by 25°F.

Baking Temperature

350°F

Timetable

Total preparation time About 3 hours

Working time 15 minutes

Kneading time About 5 minutes

First rise 1½ hours

Shaping time 15 to 20 minutes

Second rise 30 minutes

Storage

Best served at room temperature the day it is made. Or, store wrapped in plastic in the refrigerator for up to 3 days, or freeze for up to 2 months (page 25).

Specific Skills

• Preparing a sweet yeast dough and a fruit-based syrup wash.
• Rolling out a sweet dough.
• Preparing a cheese filling.

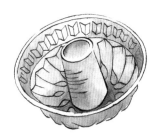

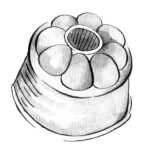

THREE FLUTED
TUBE PANS ·

2 MIXING THE DOUGH: In a large bowl using a wooden spoon or in the bowl of a heavy-duty electric mixer fitted with the paddle attachment, cream the butter with the sugar until smooth. Add the eggs, one at a time, and beat until incorporated. Add the yeast mixture, the sour cream, salt, lemon zest, and 2 cups of the flour. Beat until a smooth batter is formed, about 2 minutes. Add the remaining flour, ½ cup at a time, to form a soft dough that just clears the sides of the bowl.

3 KNEADING: Turn the dough out onto a lightly floured work surface and knead until a very soft, springy dough is formed, 1 to 3 minutes for a machine-mixed dough and 4 to 7 minutes for a hand-mixed dough, dusting with flour only 1 tablespoon at a time, just enough as needed to prevent sticking. This dough is very rich and does not require a long kneading time; it can easily absorb too much flour. Take care to keep the dough as soft as possible. Place in a greased deep container, turn once to coat the top, and cover with plastic wrap. Let rise at room temperature until doubled in bulk, about 1½ hours.

4 PREPARING THE CHEESE FILLING: In a medium bowl with a wooden spoon or the electric mixer, beat the cheeses until smooth. Add the sugar and beat until fluffy. Add the eggs, one at a time, beating well after each addition. Add the lemon juice. Refrigerate until needed.

5 SHAPING AND FILLING: Turn the dough out onto the work surface. Brush the 2 mini bundt pans with melted butter. Divide the dough in half. With a rolling pin, roll 1 portion of the dough into a 12-inch circle about ½ to ¾ inch thick. Fold in half and place over half of the prepared pan. Unfold the dough and carefully fit it into the bottom with 2 to 3 inches of dough hanging over the edge of the mold. The center tube will be covered by the dough. Repeat with the other portion of dough and other pan. Divide cheese filling between the 2 pans and spread to even. Lift overhanging dough back over the filling and place in overlapping folds to cover it. Press the folded edges against the inside tube to encase the filling. With kitchen shears, cut an X in the dough covering the center tube. Fold each triangle back over the folds of dough. Repeat with the second pan. Cover loosely with plastic wrap and set aside at room temperature to rise for 30 minutes, or until dough comes to ¼ inch below top rim of the pans.

6 BAKING OFF, COOLING, AND GLAZING: Preheat the oven to 350°F. Bake in the center of the oven for 35 to 40 minutes, or until quite brown and a cake tester inserted in the center comes out clean. Let cool in the pan for 10 minutes. Turn out onto a wire rack. While the cake is cooling in the pan, prepare the glaze. Combine the jam and brandy in a small saucepan and heat to boiling. After turning the cake out of the pan, immediately brush the glaze over the entire surface of the warm pastry two times. Let cool for at least 1 hour before slicing.

Baker's Notes While rolling and laying the dough into the pan, take care not to break the dough; if it does break, pinch it closed to encase the filling. ◆ It is important to grease the fine creases in the pan's fluted sides to avoid sticking. ◆ The ring shape of the pan promotes even heat distribution into the center of the bread during baking. ◆ You may substitute reduced fat sour cream, if desired.

Savory Cheese Turnovers

Unlike the Italian calzone turnover this is fashioned after, this meal-in-a-crust is made with a simple egg dough mixed by the straight method rather than a lean pizza dough. It makes a puffy cheese bread that is a favorite for picnics. It belongs to a large family of rustic savory pastries that includes Indian samosas, Cornish pasties, French chaussons, and Russian pirozhki. Pay attention to the sealing technique to keep the filling secure.

BAKING TIME 30 TO 35 MINUTES

Dough

1 tablespoon (1 package) active dry yeast

Pinch of granulated sugar

¾ cup warm water (105° to 115°F)

½ cup warm milk (105° to 115°F)

¼ cup olive oil

¼ cup (½ stick) unsalted butter, at room temperature, cut into pieces

2 eggs

2½ teaspoons salt

¼ cup yellow cornmeal or polenta

1 cup semolina flour

3¼ to 3¾ cups unbleached all-purpose or high-gluten bread flour

Olive oil, for brushing

2 tablespoons sesame seeds

Cheese Filling

1 pound whole-milk mozzarella, diced

1 pound Italian Fontina, diced

4 ounces domestic or imported fresh goat cheese, such as Chabi or Montrachet, crumbled

½ cup drained and chopped oil-packed sundried tomatoes

1 PROOFING THE YEAST: In a small bowl or 1 cup liquid measure, sprinkle the yeast and sugar over ¼ cup of the warm water. Stir to dissolve and let stand until foamy, about 10 minutes.

2 MIXING THE DOUGH: In a large bowl using a whisk or in the bowl of a heavy-duty electric mixer fitted with the paddle attachment, combine the remaining water, milk, olive oil, butter, eggs, salt, cornmeal, semolina flour, and ½ cup of the unbleached flour. Beat hard until creamy, about 1 minute. Stir in the yeast mixture. Beat for 1

Appearance

This is a soft bread with a firm, even texture; it encases a pale melted cheese filling and is topped with seeds. The crumb is cream colored flecked with gold. The crisp golden brown crust softens as it stands. The turnovers easily hold their shape when sliced. The flavor is mildly tangy.

Equipment

Small, medium, and large (at least 6-quart) mixing bowls

Measuring spoons and cups

Large balloon whisk and wooden spoon

Heavy-duty electric mixer with flat paddle attachment or dough hook (optional)

Plastic and metal dough scrapers

Dough container, preferably a 6-quart deep plastic container

Rolling pin

Pastry brush

Large metal spatula

Cooling rack

Serrated knife for slicing

Baking Pans and Yield

Two large turnover-shaped loaves using 1 greased or parchment-lined 11-by-16-inch baking sheet.

Baking Temperature

400°F

Timetable

Total preparation time About 3 hours

Working time 15 minutes

Kneading time About 5 minutes

First rise 1 to 1¼ hours

Shaping time 15 to 20 minutes

Second rise 15 minutes

BAKED TURNOVER
SHAPE ·

minute. Add the remaining flour, ½ cup at a time, until a shaggy dough that clears the sides of the bowl is formed. Switch to a wooden spoon as necessary if making by hand.

3 KNEADING: Turn the dough out onto a lightly floured surface and knead until the dough is smooth and satiny, 1 to 3 minutes for a machine-mixed dough and 4 to 7 minutes for a hand-mixed dough, dusting with flour only 1 tablespoon at a time, just enough as needed to prevent sticking. The dough will not be sticky, but it will still be soft.

4 FIRST RISE AND PREPARING THE CHEESE FILLING: Place the dough in a greased deep container, turn once to coat the top, and cover with plastic wrap. Let rise at room temperature until double in bulk, about 1 to 1¼ hours. While the dough is rising, prepare the cheese filling. In a medium bowl, combine the mozzarella, Fontina, goat cheese, and sundried tomatoes. Toss to combine evenly and set aside.

5 SHAPING, FILLING, AND SECOND RISE: Grease or parchment-line the baking sheet. Gently deflate the dough, turn it out onto a lightly floured work surface, and divide into 2 equal portions. With a rolling pin, roll out each portion into a 12-by-15-inch oval. Drape the dough over the rolling pin and place the dough on the baking sheet. Sprinkle half the cheese filling on the bottom half of the long side of the oval, leaving a 2-inch rim around the bottom edge, mounding the cheese in the center. Moisten the edge with water and fold the top of the oval over the filled bottom to form a half-moon shape with the edges meeting even. Pinch the edges to seal and enclose the filling securely. Starting with the top edge, fold a section of the dough over itself and continue to fold in sections to form a ropelike edge, pinching at regular intervals. Or seal with the tines of a fork. Roll out, fill, and form the second turnover. Prick the tops for steam vents. Brush some olive oil gently over the top of the turnovers and sprinkle each with sesame seeds. Let the loaves rest at room temperature, uncovered, for 15 minutes while preheating the oven to 400°F.

6 BAKING OFF AND COOLING: Bake the turnovers in the center of the oven for 30 to 35 minutes, or until puffed and golden brown. Let the turnovers stand 5 minutes before transferring with a large metal spatula to a cooling rack. Let cool for at least 30 minutes. Serve warm, sliced using a serrated knife.

Baker's Notes Pleat or crimp the outer edge carefully to avoid leakage during baking. ◆ It's best to fill the turnover on the pan, as transferring the finished product can result in stretching and breaking the dough. ◆ Substitute ½ cup of chopped black olives or, for a very special occasion, a few precious slices of a black truffle in season (December) for the sundried tomatoes.

Pecan Brioche

Pecan Brioche is my winter indulgence. It is a tender double-swirled nut loaf so divine and rich tasting that you could become famous solely by baking this bread. This classic and butter-rich French-style dough was taught to me by chef and baker Donna Nordin just as she had learned to make it at the prestigious Cordon Bleu cooking school. It was both a revelation and revolution in terms of technique. An often tricky, complicated, and time-consuming manual task is transformed into a foolproof one by means of a heavy-duty electric mixer. The ever-so-rich, very soft dough never comes in contact with the heat of your hands; this avoids melting as well as the friction of laborious hand mixing. Since the high fat content inhibits fermentation, the dough must be carefully mixed to ensure the even distribution of ingredients. The dough is constructed with the rapid-mix (page 19) and CoolRise method (see page 28); it must be refrigerated overnight to firm it up enough for handling during filling and shaping, so plan to make the dough the day before you bake it.

BAKING TIME 40 TO 45 MINUTES

4½ cups unbleached all-purpose flour, exact measure

Grated zest of 1 orange

1 tablespoon (1 package) active dry yeast

¼ cup granulated sugar

2 teaspoons salt

½ cup hot water (120°F)

6 eggs, at room temperature

1 cup (2 sticks) unsalted butter, at room temperature, cut into small pieces

Pecan Paste

4 tablespoons (½ stick) unsalted butter, at room temperature

¾ cup (packed) light brown sugar

1 egg

1 teaspoon pure vanilla extract

2 cups finely chopped pecans

1 tablespoon unsalted butter, melted, for brushing

Appearance
This is a light, rich bread dotted with small air pockets and an attractive scroll line of nut paste swirling throughout the bread. It has a crisp dark brown hairline thin crust that softens as it stands. The flavor is ambrosial and the texture delicate.

Equipment
Measuring spoons and cups
Heavy-duty electric mixer with flat paddle attachment or dough hook
Rubber spatula
Plastic and metal dough scrapers
Dough container, preferably a 6-quart deep plastic container
Rolling pin
Pastry brush
Cooling rack

Baking Pans and Yield
Two loaves using standard 9-by-5-inch metal, nonstick, glass, or disposable aluminum loaf pans, greased on all inside surfaces. If using glass or black-finish aluminum pans, reduce heat by 25°F.

Baking Temperature
350°F

Timetable
Total preparation time About 6½ hours, divided over 2 days
Working time 15 minutes
First rise 3 hours
Second rise 12 to 24 hours
Shaping time 15 to 20 minutes
Third rise 2 to 2½ hours

1 MIXING THE DOUGH: In the bowl of a heavy-duty mixer fitted with a paddle attachment, combine 1 cup of the flour, the orange zest, yeast, sugar, and salt. Add the hot water and beat at medium speed for 2 minutes, or until smooth. Add the eggs, one at a time, beating well after each addition. Gradually beat in 2 more cups of the flour. When well blended, add the butter, a few pieces at a time. Beat just until completely incorporated. Reduce the speed to low and gradually add the remaining 1½ cups flour. Beat until thoroughly blended and creamy in consistency. The dough will be very soft and batterlike.

2 FIRST RISE AND OVERNIGHT REFRIGERATED REST: With a spatula or plastic dough scraper, scrape the dough into a greased deep container. Cover tightly with plastic wrap and let rise at cool room temperature until double in bulk, about 3 hours. Gently deflate the dough with the spatula or plastic dough scraper, cover tightly, and refrigerate for 12 hours or as long as 24 hours.

3 PREPARING THE PECAN PASTE: In the bowl of the electric mixer, cream the butter and brown sugar. Add the egg and beat until smooth. Add the vanilla and the nuts and beat until evenly combined. Set aside.

4 SHAPING, FILLING, AND FINAL RISE: Grease the 9-by-5-inch loaf pans. Turn out the chilled dough onto a lightly floured work surface and divide it into 2 equal portions. Roll each portion into a rectangle about 12-by-8 inches. Spread each rectangle evenly with half of the pecan paste, leaving a 1-inch border all the way around the edge. Working from both long sides at the same time, tightly roll up each rectangle to meet in the center, forming 2 tight scroll-like swirls. Turn the loaves over and place each in a loaf pan. Lightly brush the top with melted butter. Cover with plastic wrap and let rise at cool room temperature until puffy and double in bulk, 2 to 2½ hours.

5 BAKING OFF AND COOLING: Twenty minutes before baking, preheat the oven to 350°F. Bake in the center of the oven for 40 to 45 minutes, or until the loaves are golden brown and firm to the touch; a cake tester inserted into the center should come out clean. Let stand in the pans for 5 minutes. Remove the loaves from the pans and transfer to a rack to cool completely before slicing.

Baker's Notes Brioche is most familiar shaped into a round roll with a jaunty topknot known as *brioche à tête*. Brioche dough is also traditionally used for encasing brie cheese rounds and sausages. ◆ All rising periods for the brioche dough must be at cool room temperatures. The butter will separate from the dough if it is risen in the traditional "warm place" called for in most bread recipes. ◆ Brioche dough may be made by hand in the time-honored tradition of European bakers. For specific directions for making it directly on the bench with the well method, which was taught to me in the manner of the French chef and teacher Madeleine Kamman, please refer to the technique detailed in my book *Baking Bread* (Chronicle Books, 1992).

Storage

Pecan Brioche is best eaten the day it is made, but it makes excellent day-old toast. Store the unsliced bread wrapped in a plastic food storage bag at room temperature for up to 3 days, or freeze (page 25). Reheat as needed.

Specific Skills

◆ Mixing a rich dough. ◆ Addition and incorporation of butter pieces. ◆ Further work with retarded doughs. ◆ Preparing a nut paste. ◆ Shaping and filling the scroll from chilled dough. ◆ Attention to temperature during fermentation.

DOUGH ROLLED FROM BOTH LONG SIDES INTO THE CENTER.

Braid of Fruit

A good all-purpose sweet dough has a place in every baker's repertoire. All sweet doughs are minor variations of the same basic proportions, although the fillings and shapes vary. Sweet doughs are higher in fat and sugar than daily loaf breads, though not as rich as the brioche, and these contribute to a sumptuous taste and texture. The butter is incorporated in small pieces in the manner of creaming, utilizing a modified straight-dough method. Baking a coffee cake—type bread is more artistically rewarding than baking a plain loaf, as the contrast of colors and sculpting of the dough make for a visually beautiful product. The shape of this coffee cake is known as a false plait; it is one of my favorite methods of shaping a coffee cake to showcase a cooked fruit filling. It's lots easier to form than a three-strand braid and it securely contains the filling. Each of the fruit filling recipes that follow the main recipe will fill the two braids. Your kitchen will fill with a delicate perfume while this bread is baking.

BAKING TIME 35 TO 40 MINUTES

Sponge

1½ tablespoons (1½ packages) active dry yeast

1 tablespoon granulated sugar

¼ cup warm water (105° to 115°F)

1¼ cups warm milk (105° to 115°F)

2 cups unbleached all-purpose or high-gluten bread flour

Dough

2 large eggs

Finely grated zest of 1 lemon or orange

2 teaspoons salt

⅓ cup granulated sugar

2½ to 3 cups unbleached all-purpose or high-gluten bread flour

¾ cup (1½ sticks) unsalted butter at room temperature, cut into small pieces

Fruit filling (recipes follow)

Streusel Crumb Topping

½ cup sugar

Grated zest of 1 lemon or orange

1 teaspoon ground cinnamon

⅓ cup unbleached all-purpose flour

4 tablespoons (½ stick) cold unsalted butter, cut into pieces

Appearance

Long rectangular fruit-filled braids topped with a layer of light brown crumbs. The dough has a dense, even texture, a soft cakelike crumb, and a soft crust.

Equipment

Small, medium, and large (at least 6-quart) mixing bowls
Measuring spoons and cups
Large balloon whisk and wooden spoon
Heavy-duty electric mixer with flat paddle attachment or dough hook (optional)
Plastic and metal dough scrapers
Dough container, preferably a 6-quart deep plastic container
Medium saucepan
Rolling pin
Rubber spatula
Chef's knife or pastry wheel
Pastry cutter or food processor
Wide metal spatula
Cooling rack
Immersion blender or food mill

Baking Pans and Yield

Two 15-inch-long braided breads using 1 or 2 greased or parchment-lined 11-by-16-inch baking sheets.

Baking Temperature

350°F

Timetable

Total preparation time About 4 hours, divided over 2 days
Sponge fermentation 30 minutes
Working time 15 minutes
Kneading time About 7 minutes
First rise 1½ to 2 hours
Second rise 12 to 24 hours
Shaping time 15 to 20 minutes
Third rise 45 minutes

CUTTING ALONG
OUTSIDE EDGE.

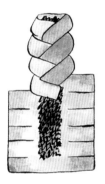

FOLDING STRIPS
OVER
THE FILLING.

1 PREPARING THE SPONGE: In a large bowl with a whisk or the bowl of a heavy-duty electric mixer fitted with the paddle attachment, combine the yeast, sugar, water, milk, and 2 cups of flour. Beat hard until smooth, about 1 minute. Cover with plastic wrap and let rest at room temperature for 30 minutes, or until bubbly.

2 PREPARING THE DOUGH: Add the eggs, zest, salt, sugar, and 1 cup of flour to the sponge. Beat until smooth. Add the butter, a few pieces at a time, and beat until incorporated. Add the remaining flour, ¼ cup at a time, to form a soft dough that just clears the sides of the bowl. Switch to a wooden spoon when necessary if making by hand. The dough must be very soft.

3 KNEADING, FIRST RISE, AND OVERNIGHT REST: Turn the dough out onto a lightly floured work surface and knead until smooth, shiny, and soft, 1 to 3 minutes for a machine-mixed dough and 4 to 7 minutes for a hand-mixed dough, dusting with flour only 1 tablespoon at a time, just enough as needed to prevent sticking. This dough must remain very soft and pliable. Place in a greased deep container, turn once to coat the top, and cover with plastic wrap. Let rise at room temperature until double in bulk, about 1½ to 2 hours. Gently deflate the dough, re-cover, and refrigerate for 12 to 24 hours. Prepare the fruit filling and refrigerate, covered, until needed.

4 SHAPING, FILLING, AND SECOND RISE: Grease or parchment-line 1 or 2 baking sheets. Turn the dough out onto a lightly floured work surface and divide into 2 equal portions. Roll out each portion with a rolling pin into an 8-by-12-inch rectangle. Gently transfer the dough to the baking sheet and even out the rectangular shape. Spread half the fruit filling down the center third of each rectangle. With a sharp knife or pastry wheel, cut diagonal strips at 2-inch intervals down the outside portions of the dough, almost through to the filling. Starting at the top, fold the strips over the filling alternately from each side at a slight angle. The strips will overlap slightly. If there is any excess at the bottom, tuck it under. Cover loosely with plastic wrap and let rise at room temperature until double in bulk, about 45 minutes. A three-quarter proof is best for this dough.

5 PREPARING THE STREUSEL CRUMBS: While the dough is finishing its second rise, prepare the streusel. In a small bowl, combine the sugar, zest, cinnamon, and flour. Cut in the butter pieces with your fingers, a fork, or a food processor until coarse crumbs are formed. Set aside.

6 BAKING OFF AND COOLING: Twenty minutes before baking, preheat the oven to 350°F. Sprinkle the surface of the braids with the streusel crumbs. Bake the loaves in the center of the oven until the filling is bubbly and the crust is golden brown and firm to the touch, 35 to 40 minutes. Gently remove from the pan, with a wide metal spatula if necessary, to cool completely on a rack.

Berry Filling

2 cups fresh or unthawed frozen unsweetened raspberries, blackberries, boysenberries, gooseberries, or
      olallieberries

¼ to ½ cup sugar, or to taste

¼ cup cornstarch

2 tablespoons fresh lemon juice, or berry liqueur, such as Chambord, or golden rum

In a medium saucepan, combine all the filling ingredients and bring to a boil. Lower the heat and simmer until the fruit juices are thick, stirring occasionally and gently to keep the berries as whole as possible. Remove from the heat and set aside to cool. Refrigerate until needed.

Prune or Apricot Filling

3 cups pitted dried prunes or apricots

¼ cup sugar

4 tablespoons (½ stick) unsalted butter

3 tablespoons fresh orange juice or good-quality brandy

In a small saucepan, place the prunes or apricots with water to cover. Bring to a boil and simmer, uncovered, until tender, about 15 minutes. Drain. Purée until smooth and fluffy with a food mill or with a food processor. Beat in the sugar, butter, and orange juice until combined and the butter is melted. Refrigerate until needed.

Maple-Blueberry Filling

1 pint (2 cups) fresh blueberries or 1 package (16 ounces) unthawed frozen unsweetened blueberries

¼ cup pure maple syrup

¼ cup cornstarch

2 tablespoons fresh lemon juice

In a medium saucepan, combine all the ingredients and bring to a boil. Lower the heat and simmer until the blueberry juices are thick, stirring occasionally and gently to keep the berries as whole as possible. Remove from the heat and let cool to room temperature. Refrigerate until needed.

Fresh Pineapple Filling

2 small or 1 large whole fresh pineapple (total weight 3 to 4 pounds), peeled, cored, and chopped

1½ cups sugar

2 tablespoons fresh lemon juice

4 teaspoons pure vanilla extract

In a medium saucepan, combine the pineapple, sugar, and lemon juice, and bring to a low boil. Lower the heat and simmer until the juices are almost evaporated and the mixture is thick, stirring frequently. Remove from the heat, mix in the vanilla, and let cool to room temperature. Refrigerate until needed.

Rich sweet doughs with a fruit filling have a good shelf life and do not stale quickly, staying moist about 3 days. Store the unsliced braid in the refrigerator wrapped in a plastic food storage bag, or freeze (page 25) and reheat before serving.

Specific Skills
• Mixing a rich and sweet yeast straight dough. • Preparing streusel crumbs and cooked fruit fillings. • Rolling out a sweet dough. • Shaping and filling a large false plait loaf.

Cranberry-Orange Filling

This filling is also excellent made with port wine substituted for the orange juice and zest.

>   3 cups fresh cranberries
>   ⅔ cup sugar
>   ⅔ cup dried cranberries
>   ⅓ cup orange juice
>   Grated zest of 2 oranges

In a medium saucepan, combine all the ingredients and bring to a boil. Lower the heat and simmer until the cranberry juices are thick, stirring occasionally. Remove from the heat and let cool to room temperature. Refrigerate until needed.

Fresh Apple Filling

Here apples are layered on top of a classic butter-and-sugar pastry cream filling, also known as remonce.

>   1 cup (2 sticks) unsalted butter, at room temperature
>   1 cup granulated sugar or 1¼ cups (packed) light brown sugar
>   1½ teaspoons pure vanilla extract
>   1 teaspoon ground cinnamon, nutmeg, or cardamom
>   3 to 4 large cooking apples, peeled, cored, and sliced thin

In a small bowl, cream the butter, sugar, and vanilla together until smooth. Refrigerate until needed, but bring to room temperature before spreading. Spread half of the pastry cream down the center third of each dough rectangle. Arrange the apples in overlapping slices down the center over the butter mixture and form the braid as directed. The pastry cream may be made 1 week in advance.

Baker's Notes Make certain the fruit filling is at room temperature or cold before filling, or the dough will become soggy. ◆ Take care to not overmix the streusel crumbs; they will easily form a paste. ◆ This soft dough needs the overnight rest to become firm enough for rolling out properly. ◆ Most fillings can be made 1 day in advance with the exception of the Fresh Apple Filling, which can be made 1 week in advance.

Danish Pastries

Known as Kopenhagener Wienerbrot *in Austria and* Viennabröd *(Vienna bread) in Denmark, these artistically formed individual pastries are a favorite bakery item across America as well as in Europe. The rolling and folding techniques necessary for the multitude of flaky layers are the same as those used in the Italian* pasta sfogliata *(literally leaved dough) and French croissant pastry. Although the technique may seem daunting, it is easily mastered, and the homemade baked pastries make this labor of love worth every minute in the kitchen. Resist the impulse to be overcritical of your shaping if it's uneven or imperfect, as the rising and baking will correct most irregularities, and your personal style will develop with practice. The most important advice in working with a folded dough is to keep the dough and butter cold every step of the way. Remember also that the dough is mixed and turned the day before shaping and baking. Fillings range from nut to fruit to cheese. I have included directions for my favorites, but mix and match them as you like, or use a can of prune, nut, or poppy seed paste, if that is to your taste. These hand-formed pastries will be smaller in size than most commercial bakery Danish. I learned how to make these pastries from master baker Diane Dexter at Tante Marie's Cooking School in San Francisco.*

BAKING TIME 15 TO 25 MINUTES, DEPENDING ON THE SIZE AND SHAPE

1½ tablespoons (1½ packages) active dry yeast

¼ cup (packed) light brown sugar

¼ cup warm water (105° to 115°F)

1 cup half-and-half, light cream, or whole milk, very cold

½ cup (1 stick) unsalted butter, melted

2 eggs

1 teaspoon salt

Grated zest of 1 orange

½ teaspoon ground mace or cardamom

1 teaspoon pure vanilla extract

4½ cups unbleached all-purpose flour, divided

1½ cups (3 sticks) unsalted butter, very cold

Egg Glaze (page 118)

Fillings (recipes follow)

Finishing Glaze

½ cup sifted powdered sugar

1 tablespoon milk or cream

1 teaspoon unsalted butter, melted

¼ teaspoon lemon, orange, almond, or pure vanilla extract

Appearance

A variety of shapes with a crisp, golden brown crust and soft interior with sweet fruit, nut, or cheese fillings. The pastries should be open textured with definite stratospheres of layering.

Equipment

Small and large (at least 6-quart) mixing bowls

Measuring spoons and cups

Large balloon whisk and wooden spoon

Heavy-duty electric mixer with flat paddle attachment or dough hook (optional)

Plastic and metal dough scrapers, wide plastic spatula

Large baking sheet

Marble slab or wooden or vinyl plastic cutting board, at least 22-by-15 inches

Large heavy rolling pin, preferably roller-bearings style

Ruler or kitchen tape measure

Soft 1½-inch wide pastry brush

Chef's knife or pastry wheel

Wide plastic wrap

Cooling rack

Baking Pans and Yield

Twenty to 24 individual pastries, using two 11-by-16-inch baking sheets, lined or ungreased.

Baking Temperature

400°F

Timetable

Total preparation time About 5 hours, divided over 2 days

Working time 15 minutes

First rise 45 minutes to 1 hour

Forming the butter package 5 to 10 minutes

Layering time 2 minutes with 30 minutes of rest in between

Second rise Overnight

Shaping time 15 to 30 minutes

Third rise 1 to 1½ hours

ROLLING OUT THE
BUTTER PACKAGE.

FOLDING IN

DOUGH PACKAGE

1 PROOFING THE YEAST: In a small bowl, sprinkle the yeast and a pinch of the brown sugar over the warm water. Stir to dissolve. Let stand until foamy, about 10 minutes.

2 MIXING THE DOUGH: In a large bowl with a whisk or in the bowl of a heavy-duty electric mixer fitted with the paddle attachment, combine the remaining brown sugar, the half-and-half or milk, melted butter, eggs, salt, orange zest, mace, and vanilla. Beat until smooth, about 1 minute. Add the yeast mixture and exactly 4 cups of the flour. Stir until the dough comes together into a shaggy, moist mass and the flour is just absorbed with no dry patches. Switch to a wooden spoon when necessary if making by hand. Do not knead. Add 1 tablespoon flour at a time as needed to prevent stickiness but no more than a total of 4 tablespoons; this dough should be very soft.

3 FIRST RISE: Lightly dust an ungreased baking sheet with flour. Place the dough on the sheet and, using your fingers, spread the dough into a large, flat, free-form rectangle about 1 inch thick. The dough will be rough and uneven looking. Cover tightly with plastic wrap, making certain all the dough is covered, to avoid dry patches from forming. Refrigerate in the coldest part of the refrigerator until thoroughly chilled, 45 minutes to 1 hour.

4 MAKING THE BUTTER PACKAGE: Using an electric mixer, quickly combine the cold butter with the remaining ½ cup of flour until smooth and no hard lumps remain. To make by hand: Use a spatula to smear the butter on a work surface, dump the flour on top, and use a chopping motion to combine. Knead quickly until the flour is absorbed into the butter. Form the butter into a rough block on the work surface. Pat or roll quickly into a firm, fat rectangle. Wrap in plastic wrap and refrigerate if at all soft or sticky. The butter should be chilled but still pliable. This step is much easier to execute than it sounds.

5 FOLDING IN: Place the dough on a lightly floured work surface. Roll out into a 10-by-20-inch rectangle about ½ inch thick. Divide the butter mixture into 2 equal portions and roll each portion into a 6-by-8-inch rectangle. Place one of the butter portions in the middle third of the dough, working it with your fingers to have it fit. Pull a third of the dough over from the side to cover. Seal the edges to encase the butter. Place the remaining butter portion on top and fold over the remaining third of the dough. Pinch the edges together to seal completely. It is important that the butter not become too soft, or it will seep into the dough rather than form layers. Place the folded edge of the dough at on top.

6 MAKING THE FIRST TURN: Using firm strokes, roll out the dough into another large, even rectangle and fold again into thirds. Replace on the baking sheet and cover with plastic wrap. Refrigerate for at least 20 but no longer than 30 minutes to chill. If chilled longer than 30 minutes, the butter may harden too much. The chilling period allows the gluten to rest and the butter to firm to allow continued rolling.

7 MAKING THE SECOND AND THIRD TURNS: Repeat the process of rolling out and folding into thirds 2 more times to create the multilayered dough, chilling in between as needed. Take care not to tear the dough or allow the butter to get too soft. Remember to adjust the corners as you are working, to keep them square and tidy, and to move the dough constantly to avoid sticking. Use a soft brush to dust off any excess flour. Chill the dough at any point that it becomes sticky, and remember to keep the folded edge at on top.

8 OVERNIGHT REST AND SECOND RISE: Wrap the dough tightly in plastic wrap and refrigerate overnight or for up to 3 days. At this point, the dough can also be frozen for to 1 month, but fresh dough is easier to work with.

9 SHAPING AND FILLING: Line the 2 baking sheets with parchment or leave ungreased. Gently press the dough to deflate it, and cut it in half with a sharp knife in one downward motion. Do not use a sawing motion; it will destroy the delicate layering. Rewrap one section of dough and return it to the refrigerator. Place the other half of the dough on a lightly floured work surface. Roll out into a rectangle about ¼ inch thick. Keep lifting and moving the dough to prevent sticking or tearing. Roll the dough back and forth on a diagonal to achieve an even width. Trim the edges, if necessary. Cut with a sharp knife or a pastry wheel as directed for each particular shape (pages 112–115). Place the individual shapes on the baking sheets at least 2 inches apart. Do not crowd. Top with desired filling. Be careful not to put too much filling on each to avoid bubbling over during baking. At this point, the pastries may be covered with plastic wrap and left to rise in the refrigerator overnight, or frozen (page 27). Let rise, uncovered, at cool room temperature until double in bulk, 1 to 1½ hours.

10 BAKING OFF: Twenty minutes before baking, preheat the oven to 400°F. When the pastries are light and springy to the touch, brush with the egg glaze. Place a second baking sheet of the same dimensions under the one holding the pastries to double pan and prevent the bottoms from burning. Bake in the center of the oven for 15 to 25 minutes, depending on the size. To bake frozen formed Danish, remove from the freezer and place the pastries on an ungreased or parchment-lined baking sheet. Cover loosely with plastic wrap and let defrost in the refrigerator for 12 to 18 hours, or overnight. The pastries will slowly thaw and begin to rise. Remove from the refrigerator and let stand, uncovered, at room temperature for about 1 hour. Bake in the preheated oven as directed for freshly formed Danish.

11 PREPARING THE FINISHING GLAZE: In a small bowl with a whisk, combine the powdered sugar, milk, melted butter, and extract and beat until smooth and thick yet pourable. Remove hot pastries with a spatula to a rack. Glaze the pastries while hot, drizzling the glaze with the end of a spoon, a pastry bag fitted with a small plain tip, or the tips of your fingers. The glaze will set as it cools. Let the pastries cool on the racks for 15 minutes before eating.

Whole Wheat Danish Pastries

Substitute 3 cups whole wheat pastry flour for an equal amount of the all-purpose flour. Proceed as directed to mix, shape, and bake.

Sweet Cheese Danish

This envelope shape is also known as Spandauer. *The creamy filling may be varied by substituting fresh soft goat cheese, neufchatel, or a well-drained homemade yogurt cheese for half of the cream cheese.*

MAKES 12 PASTRIES AND ABOUT 1¼ CUPS FILLING

8 ounces cream cheese, whole-milk ricotta, or farmer's cheese

¼ cup granulated sugar

1½ tablespoons unbleached all-purpose flour

1 teaspoon pure vanilla extract

1 large egg yolk

Grated zest of 1 lemon

½ recipe Danish Pastry

PREPARING THE CHEESE MIXTURE: In a bowl with a spoon or with an electric mixer, beat the cheese, sugar, flour, vanilla, egg yolk, and lemon zest together until smooth and well combined. Cover and chill for at least 1 hour. The filling may be made 24 hours ahead.

SHAPING, FILLING, AND BAKING OFF THE PASTRY: On a lightly floured work surface, roll out the chilled pastry into a 12-by-16-by-¼-inch rectangle. With a sharp knife or pastry wheel, cut lengthwise into 3 equal strips, then cut each strip into 4-inch squares. Spoon about 1 heaping tablespoon of the cheese filling into the center of each square. Fold one corner of the square over the center of the filling and then fold the others over. Seal with a bit of water. Let rise and bake as directed in Step 10.

Prune Crescents

Use this basic recipe to make other dried fruit fillings by substituting an equal amount of dried apricots, cherries, dates, or figs.

MAKES 12 PASTRIES AND ABOUT 1½ CUPS FILLING

1 cup finely cut pitted dried prunes (8 ounces)

⅓ cup orange juice, prune juice, or water

¼ cup granulated sugar

1 tablespoon fresh lemon juice

½ recipe Danish Pastry

PREPARING THE PRUNE MIXTURE: In a small heavy saucepan, combine the prunes, orange juice, sugar, and lemon juice. Simmer, uncovered, until the fruit has absorbed the liquid, about 20 minutes. Remove from the heat and cool before using. The filling may be made 48 hours ahead and refrigerated.

SHAPING, FILLING, AND BAKING OFF THE PASTRIES: On a lightly floured work surface, roll out the chilled pastry into a 10-by-16-by-¼-inch rectangle. With a sharp knife or pastry wheel, cut into six 5-inch squares and then cut each square on the diagonal to make 2 triangles. Place 2 tablespoons of prune filling on the center of the base of each triangle. Roll up from the base edge and then curve the ends to form a crescent. Let rise and bake as directed in Step 10.

Blueberry Danish Turnovers

Flaky confiture-filled pastry triangles are long-time favorites of both the French and Austrian bakers. These turnovers can also be made from croissant dough.

MAKES 9 TURNOVERS

About 1¼ cups whole-fruit blueberry preserves

½ recipe Danish Pastry

SHAPING, FILLING, AND BAKING OFF THE PASTRIES: On a lightly floured work surface, roll out the chilled pastry into a 15-by-15-by-¼-inch rectangle. With a sharp knife or pastry wheel, cut into three 5-inch-wide strips and then cut each strip into three 5-inch squares. Place a generous 2 tablespoons of preserves onto the center of each square. Moisten the edges with water and fold in half on the diagonal to make a triangle. Crimp the edges with a fork to seal, and pierce the surface with a knife in 2 places to allow steam to escape. Let rise and bake as directed in Step 10.

Almond Crests

These are also known as cockscombs, lion's paws, bear's claws, or imperial crowns. In commercial bakeries the secret ingredient for extending the filling is dry cake and pastry crumbs. Walnuts, pecans, or hazelnuts can be used in place of the almonds.

MAKES 9 PASTRIES AND ABOUT 1 CUP FILLING

1 cup whole almonds

⅓ cup zwieback, biscotti, or shortbread cookie crumbs

⅓ cup (packed) light brown sugar

4 tablespoons (½ stick) unsalted butter, melted

1 egg white

½ teaspoon pure almond extract

½ recipe Danish Pastry

PREPARING THE ALMOND PASTE: Grind the nuts until coarse in a food processor. Add the remaining ingredients except the pastry and process just until a paste is formed.

SHAPING, FILLING, AND BAKING OFF THE PASTRIES: On a lightly floured work surface, roll out the chilled pastry into a 12-by-18-by-¼-inch rectangle. With a sharp knife or pastry wheel, cut into three 6-inch-wide strips, then cut each strip into three 6-inch squares. Spread a thin layer of nut paste along the center of the bottom half, leaving a full ½-inch border around the 3 sides. Fold up the bottom third of the dough over the filling and then fold the top third section over the center to completely enclose the filling. Using a sharp knife, cut ¾-inch-deep slits into the folded edge to make 2 equal-distanced slits, cutting only halfway to the opposite side. Curve slightly to form the claws on the baking sheet. Let rise and bake as directed in Step 10.

Apple Danish

Follow this recipe to make other fruit fillings by substituting firm fresh cooking pears or plums for the apples.

MAKES 10 PASTRIES AND ABOUT 1½ CUPS FILLING

4 tablespoons (½ stick) unsalted butter

2½ cups sliced and peeled tart cooking apples (about 4 medium apples)

⅓ cup (packed) light brown sugar

1 tablespoon fresh lemon juice

½ teaspoon ground cinnamon

½ recipe Danish Pastry

Spice Crumbs

½ cup granulated sugar

⅓ cup unbleached all-purpose flour

½ teaspoon ground cinnamon

4 tablespoons (½ stick) cold unsalted butter, cut into pieces

PREPARING THE APPLE MIXTURE: In a medium skillet, melt the butter over medium heat and add the apples. Cook until apples just begin to soften, 2 to 3 minutes, stirring occasionally. Add the brown sugar, lemon juice, and cinnamon and stir until the sugar dissolves. Let cool or refrigerate for up to 24 hours before using.

SHAPING, FILLING, AND BAKING OFF THE PASTRIES: On a lightly floured work surface, roll out the chilled pastry into a 10-by-16-by-¼-inch rectangle. With a sharp knife or pastry wheel, cut lengthwise into 1-inch-wide strips. With your palms on each end of a strip, twist one in the opposite direction from the other at the same time. Form a pinwheel. Tuck the tail underneath. Using your fingertips, press on the center to form an indentation for the filling. Place about 2 tablespoons of the apple filling in the center. Combine the spice crumb ingredients in a small bowl and rub the ingredients together with your fingers to make coarse crumbs. Sprinkle each pastry with a generous tablespoon of crumbs to finish. Let rise and bake as directed in Step 10.

Specific Skills
• Preparing a rich roll-in dough.
• Preparing a variety of fillings.
• Attention to temperature, retardations, and roll-out techniques. • Cutting with a pastry wheel and hand-forming techniques (bench management) in preparation for filling. • Attention to fermentation periods that are different than for bread doughs. • Baking and arranging pastries in the oven.
• Applying a simple icing.
• Comparison of roll-in dough to a straight or sponge dough.

More Bread Baking Basics

Basic Finishing Glazes and Washes

GLAZING OR WASHING IS USUALLY THE FINAL STEP after slashing the surface of a loaf before it is placed in the oven. This is totally optional, depending on the look you like your bread to have. A protein-rich egg wash, also known as a baker's varnish, is typically used by bakers to produce a finished-looking shiny top surface coating, to prevent excess drying, and to hold on nuts, seeds, candied peels, herbs, grain flakes, unprocessed bran, or rolled oats. The fatty yolk produces a dark crust and is often used on breads rich in fat and sugar. The beaten white makes a totally translucent, shiny light-brown finish for lean doughs, such as French or Italian breads, although these may also be brushed with plain water for crisping. Milk and cream contribute a dark shiny finish and soften the crust. Fats such as melted butter and oils can be brushed on a homestyle loaf at any point before, during, or after baking, to keep the crust soft and shiny and add a hint of flavor. Garlic- or herb-infused oils also work nicely, especially on savory breads, pizzas, and focaccia. When applying washes, use a soft-bristled, clean pastry brush to apply egg glazes, taking care not to puncture or deflate the loaf and not to allow the egg to drip down into the sides of the pan, which results in sticking. Egg glazes may be applied before, during, and just after baking, as directed in specific recipes. Dusting with flour, or a combination of ground spice and flour, gives an earthy matte finish.

Sweet doughs are usually drizzled with a viscous powdered-sugar icing as a flavor enhancer. Sweet breads can also be sprinkled with crushed white or brown sugar cubes, colored sugar crystals, or pearl sugar, to give a crystal-like brightness to the crust. Save your dried-up whole vanilla beans and pulverize them in a blender or food processor with some granulated sugar and keep in a tightly closed jar especially for sprinkling. A splash of brandy or some other liqueur is a very special flavor enhancer for powdered sugar icings. Always on my pantry shelf is a small bottle of good cognac in which I have placed three vanilla beans; it's a cross between a liqueur and a premium vanilla extract. Warm honey, maple syrup, or molasses soften the surface and add a glistening sweetness when combined with an equal amount of warm water. These toppings are most dramatic when their flavors complement some of the ingredients used to compose the dough.

Egg Glaze

For crusty French- and Italian-style lean country breads to give a shine without browning.

1 egg white

1 tablespoon water

Dash salt

In a small bowl with a mini whisk or fork, beat the ingredients together until foamy. Use immediately.

Rich Egg Glaze

For American-style pan loaves, Jewish Egg Bread, sweet breads, dinner rolls, and brioche to give a bright shine and medium brown color.

1 yolk or 1 whole egg

1 tablespoon water, milk, or cream

In a small bowl with a mini whisk or fork, beat the ingredients together until well combined. Use immediately or refrigerate until needed.

Egg Yolk Glaze

For sweet and savory pan loaves and dinner rolls to give a deep golden brown shine.

1 egg yolk

2 tablespoons water

In a small bowl with a mini-whisk or fork, beat the ingredients together until foamy. Use immediately.

Sweet Egg Glaze

For American-style sweet loaf breads, sweet breakfast buns, raisin and sweet egg breads, and brioche to give a bright shine and dark brown color.

1 whole egg

1½ teaspoons sugar

In a small bowl with a mini whisk or fork, beat the ingredients together until foamy. Use immediately.

Oil Wash

For savory loaves, dinner rolls, and tortas.

1 whole egg

2 teaspoons olive, nut, or vegetable oil

In a small bowl with a mini whisk or fork, beat the ingredients together until well combined. Use immediately.

Bittersweet Chocolate Glaze

For sweet breads and brioche.

> 6 ounces semisweet chocolate chips or chopped bittersweet chocolate
>
> ½ cup (1 stick) unsalted butter
>
> 1 tablespoon corn syrup

In the top portion of a double boiler, combine all the ingredients and melt slowly over simmering water. Stir occasionally. Remove from the heat as soon as melted and let stand at room temperature, or chill briefly, to a thick, pourable consistency. Pour the glaze over a barely warm loaf, allowing the glaze to drip down the sides. Let stand for at least 4 hours before slicing. The glaze will set up as it stands. Enough for 1 oversized braid, 2 large loaves, or about 16 little brioches.

Powdered Sugar Glaze

A pourable, shiny, cream-colored icing for use on sweet breads and rolls. If topping the loaf with whole and/or chopped nuts, sprinkle while the icing is moist; it will set up and any embellishments will adhere as it dries. Glaze as directed in each recipe, usually when the loaf is still slightly warm but not hot. If a loaf is to be frozen, glaze after defrosting.

> 1 cup sifted powdered sugar
>
> 1 tablespoon unsalted butter, melted
>
> 2 to 3 tablespoons milk or cream, spirits or liqueur, or hot water

In a small bowl with a whisk, combine the ingredients and beat well until smooth. Adjust the consistency by adding milk, a few drops at a time. Drizzle or pour over the warm or cool bread in the desired pattern as directed. Enough for 1 oversized braid, 2 large loaves, or 2 coffee cakes.

VARIATIONS

VANILLA: Add 1 teaspoon pure vanilla extract.

ALMOND: Add ½ to 1 teaspoon pure almond extract.

MAPLE: Substitute pure maple syrup for the milk.

CITRUS: Substitute fresh or thawed frozen concentrate of lemon, orange, lime, or tangerine juice for the milk.

CHOCOLATE: Add 1 tablespoon unsweetened cocoa.

COFFEE: Add 1 teaspoon powdered instant espresso.

SPICE: Add ½ teaspoon ground cinnamon, cardamom, or nutmeg.

SPIRITS: Substitute good-quality brandy, rum, or a nut or orange liqueur for the liquid.

Troubleshooting

SOONER OR LATER EVERY BAKER ENCOUNTERS PROBLEMS inherent to the complex process of baking with yeast, from a loaf that does not rise to one that tastes like old beer. Instead of interpreting the faulty loaf as a disaster, regard it as another way of learning about handling doughs and take the steps to remedy the procedures. Double check the recipe, ingredients, and techniques for possible errors in execution. Make notes for future reference on the recipe. The most frequent problems for a beginning baker are

- Using liquid that is too hot to proof the yeast effectively
- Adding too much flour during the kneading
- Not kneading a dough well enough
- Letting the shaped loaves rise too long or not long enough in the pans

Here are some common problems with probable causes.

DOUGH WON'T RISE

Yeast was omitted or old or it was killed with too-hot liquid

Liquid too cold and yeast improperly activated

Low gluten content in flour/too high a percentage of whole-grain flour/old flour/too much flour

Dough risen in too cool a place—will rise very slowly

THICK AND TOUGH CRUST

Too much flour

Too little sugar or fat

Underfermented

Oven temperature too low during baking

FLAT TASTE

Forgot to add the salt

TEXTURE DENSE AND SOGGY

Too much liquid in proportion to the flour

Dough underkneaded

Risen too long before baking

Underbaked

TEXTURE CRUMBLY AND DRY

Flour too low in protein

Not enough liquid/too much flour

Dough underkneaded

POROUS TEXTURE AND STRONG YEAST ODOR

Too much yeast used in proportion to the flour

YEASTY TASTE AND GRAY CAST TO THE CRUMB

Too long and too warm a fermentation

Too much yeast

CHEWY AND DRY TEXTURE

Too little fat in proportion to the other ingredients

FLAT AND COMPACT PAN LOAF

Too little liquid or yeast

Flour too low in protein

Dough overfermented in the pan and then collapsed
    in the oven

Pan too large for dough volume

Oven too hot

FLAT FREEFORM LOAF

Dough was too soft to hold its shape; knead in
    more flour next time

Too high a percentage of whole grain flour

ONE SIDE HIGHER THAN THE OTHER

Uneven oven heat; rotate pans every 10 minutes

LOAF COLLAPSED DURING BAKING

Risen too long before baking

PALE BOTTOM CRUST

Not baked long enough; remove from pan and bake
5 to 10 minutes longer directly on the oven rack

PALE SIDE CRUSTS

Overfermented

Underbaked/oven temperature too low

Pans set too close together in the oven

TEXTURE HAS A LAYERED/STREAKY LOOK

Improper mixing

Insufficient kneading or molding

Dough dried out during rising

SHELLING (TOP CRUST SEPARATES)

Overmixing

Bottom seam not on the bottom

Top dried out during rising

Oven temperature too low or uneven

Too much yeast in proportion to the flour

BREAD ROSE OVER PAN SIDES

Pan too small for dough volume

FLAT TOP CRUST

Underkneaded/not enough flour

Overrisen

Equipment Checklist

THE TOOLS AND EQUIPMENT USED IN PREPARING BREAD and baking are simple. Although wonderful homemade bread can be made with a minimum of equipment—a large crockery bowl, measuring cups and spoons, a wooden spoon, a bread pan, and an oven—consider streamlining your bakery kitchen. At first glance, the following list may look daunting, but you will not be buying everything at once, and you will use what you buy for a lifetime.

Create a simple, efficient work space just for you. Have a counter laid with a marble slab or plastic board or use a wooden work table or a butcher block; avoid working on tile counters, since dough tends to stick to the grout. Have plenty of room around the work space for easy large movements and easy cleanup. Have canisters or plastic containers of flour, sugar, and salt close by. On my work table I have a ceramic crock containing the tools I need: whisks, spoons, spatulas, and dough scrapers. Next to the work area, I also have a heavy-duty electric mixer and sets of graduated mixing bowls. For cleanup, I keep a bag of plastic mesh scrubbers under the sink, the most effective tool for cleaning dough off bowls and the work space. On shelves below are pans, baking sheets, and a baking stone. In this book, each recipe lists the equipment needed for that particular recipe. The following list is a general list.

- Baguette tray pans
- Baking pans and molds: heavy aluminum, European tinned steel, glass, earthenware, or nonstick
- Baking sheets: heavy aluminum or steel in several sizes that fit in your oven
- *Bannetons,* or muslin-lined baskets for rising European-style freeform breads
- Biscuit cutters and pastry wheel
- Bowls: crockery, glass, stainless steel or aluminum, and deep plastic buckets in a variety of sizes from small to oversized, for mixing and rising
- Chef's knife, citrus grater, kitchen shears
- Cooling racks: stainless steel, wire, or wood
- Dough scrapers: 6-inch flexible plastic for scraping bowls and a stainless steel bench knife scraper with a wooden handle for cleaning the work surface and dividing pieces of dough

- Food processor
- Heavy-duty electric stand mixer with three attachments: the flat paddle, the wire whip, and the dough hook
- Heavy-duty oven mitts, to protect the lower arms
- Loaf pans in several sizes, individual or frames
- Long serrated bread knife, for slicing baked loaves, cutting sweet roll dough, and for decorative slashing before baking
- Measuring cups, liquid and dry
- Measuring spoons
- Molds: fluted brioche molds, charlotte molds, pie pans, popover pans
- Muffin tins
- Parchment paper for lining pans
- Pastry brushes: several, 1 to 3 inches wide, with natural bristles for applying glazes, and a large, clean paint brush for dusting off the work space
- Pizza pans
- Plastic wrap, in the widest width available, for covering doughs during rising
- Pullman pans
- Rolling pin, preferably the large ball-bearing type
- Scale: beam-balance, electronic, or spring
- Spatulas: plastic and metal, one extra-wide
- Spoons: wooden and metal
- Springform pans
- Tape measure
- Thermometers: oven and instant-read yeast
- Timer
- Tube pans: plain and fluted (Bundt, Turk's head, Kugelhopf, panettone, savarin ring)
- Unbleached muslin cheesecloth
- Unglazed tiles or commercial baking stone and a short-handled wooden baker's peel
- Whisks: mini, regular, and large balloon type
- Work space: wooden board, marble slab, or plastic cutting board, no smaller than 15-by-21 inches, for kneading and forming

Every bread dough is formed into either a freeform or a molded loaf. Pans give form to loaves that may not be strong enough to hold their own shape. In other words, a pan gives support as well as contributing to a loaf's visual appeal. As much care needs to be taken in forming loaves as in assembling pure, fresh ingredients to create the dough. Different sizes and shapes of molds give yeasted loaves their unique character. Like me, you are certain to have favorites. Department, hardware, and specialty stores offer an astonishing number of loaf pans from which to choose.

No matter what size pan is used, the formed dough should fill half to two-thirds of the pan. Less and you will have a flat loaf; more, and you will have an overflowing top-heavy loaf that looks awkward and is difficult to slice. Small loaf pans are often welded together in a "strap" form for easy handling, with 4 to 12 loaf sections per strap. If you tend to bake multiple loaves, investigate restaurant supply stores which carry straps in various sizes. If you have small individual pans, place them on a baking sheet during the rising and baking. This eliminates lots of awkward juggling of small hot pans.

The choice of shape and of number of loaves is your decision alone. A recipe yield is a guide, not a law, but substitute a pan that has a similar dimension or volume for best results. Keep a tape measure handy in the kitchen for measuring pans and loaf lengths. Measure a pan straight across the top and note the width from the two inside edges. Height is measured from bottom to top. To determine a pan's volume, count the number of liquid cup measures it takes to fill it to the top. You can use trial and error, or you can weigh dough portions; this scaling is the method used in professional bakeries. To calculate the proper rectangular pan, use the guide below for the flour volume in a recipe or the dough weight (weight of the raw dough weighed on a balance scale or small 5-pound kitchen or postal scale).

	Pan Size	Flour Volume	Dough Weight
Jumbo	10-by-4¼ inches	4 to 5 cups	2 pounds
Standard	9-by-5 inches	4 cups	2 pounds
Large	8½-by-4½ inches	3 cups	1½ pounds
Medium	7½-by-3½ inches	2½ cups	1 pound
Small	5½-by-3 inches	1½ cups	½ pound
Miniature	4½-by-2½ inches	¾ cup	6 ounces

In general, a recipe using 6 to 8 cups of flour will fill two 9-by-5-by-3-inch (8-cup) loaf pans, two 9-inch round pans, or make 2 or more freeform loaves; it will also fill two 9-inch fluted or plain tube pans, four 7½-by-3½-inch loaf pans or 1-pound coffee cans, six to seven 5½-by-3-inch loaf pans, or twelve to fourteen 4½-by 2½-inch loaf pans.

Seasoning or refurbishing cast-iron cookware

For seasoning new or refurbishing old cast-iron cookware, scrub the piece of cookware with liquid detergent and hot water, rinse thoroughly, and dry. Apply a coating of vegetable oil, solid vegetable shortening, or spray shortening onto all of the interior surfaces. Place the cookware in a 350°F oven and heat until smoking, taking care not to let the grease burn. Remove from the oven with heavy mitts and let cool. The cookware is now ready for use. For reseasoning, apply a light layer of spray shortening, which does not become gummy or rancid like vegetable oils and lard. The buildup of these layers of grease "sweetens" the iron and prevents sticking.

A recipe using 4 to 6 cups of flour will fill two 8½-by-4½-by-2½-inch (5½-cup) loaf pans, two 8-inch round pans, or make 2 freeform loaves, or fill two 6-inch fluted tube pans, four 5½-by-3-inch loaf pans, eight 4½-by-2½-inch loaf pans, or twelve 2½-inch muffin cups.

Baking pans come in many different kinds of materials, each with its own qualities. Consider which pans work best in your oven to produce the type of loaf you like. Since greasing or not greasing a pan can make a big difference, note the specific instructions for each recipe. Pans may also be lined with baking parchment or aluminum foil to prevent sticking and to facilitate the easy removal of loaves. Baking parchment is a very strong, stiff paper that has been treated with sulfuric acid to bond the fibers; it is heat and grease resistant, perfect for baking. Look for it in the supermarket or cookware shops. It is not the same as the parchment used for writing purposes or wax paper, which is highly flammable. Do not substitute brown paper grocery bags for baking purposes; they are now made from recycled paper, and inedible chemicals are mixed with the pulp.

Aluminum Lightweight, inexpensive, easy to clean, and the best conductor of heat for baking, aluminum often comes with a nonstick coating. The gauge, or thickness, of the pans determines their efficiency in reflecting heat. The thicker the gauge, the less likely a pan is to warp or develop hot spots. The best grade is readily available to the home baker from a restaurant supply house or reputable cookware shop. Chicago Metallic and Leyse Toro are the best brands of professional heavy-weight aluminum. Disposable aluminum pans come in many sizes, bake a beautiful loaf of bread, and can even be washed on the top rack of a dishwasher for reuse. Keep a stock on hand.

Cast iron Cast-iron loaf pans, Dutch ovens, and skillets from 6 to 18 inches in diameter all have a place in the baker's kitchen for baking pan loaves, round loaves, and sweet rolls. Old recipes call for lining cast-iron pans with 2 thicknesses of oiled heavy brown paper or lining the pan with a layer of clean maple leaves and sprinkling with cornmeal to prevent sticking. New loaf pans in this material are available in hardware stores, but if you plan to use antique cast-iron equipment, be certain to have it professionally cleaned before seasoning. Heat diffuses evenly through cast iron, but it is slow to heat up and cool down. Always wear very heavy oven mitts to prevent burns when handling this type of cookware. Cast iron needs proper seasoning before using and it is important to maintain a protective coating to keep the iron from rusting. Clean by wiping out with a damp cloth (never use a scouring pad) and drying well.

Clay Once rare, clay loaf pans are becoming more available nowadays; they make wonderful loaf breads. Whether glazed or unglazed on the inside surfaces, they are heavy and are slow, steady conductors of heat. I use the Alfred Bread Pan, made from red clay deposits in Alfred, New York. New, clean 4- to 6-inch earthenware flowerpots are often called for in recipes, but be certain to thoroughly wash and seal the porous baking surfaces before using. Always place clay pans on the lowest oven rack for the bottom of the bread to brown properly. Avoid sugary doughs, which will stick to the clay. Generally, it takes 10 minutes longer to bake a loaf in a clay pan than in a metal pan. Clay pans produce a very thick, crisp crust on both white and whole-grain loaves. Scrub with soap and water to clean, and dry completely before storing.

European tin   This nonstick alloy should not be washed with soap or in the dishwasher. Lots of pizza pans are made of this material. Follow the manufacturer's instructions for seasoning before baking to prevent discoloration and merciless sticking. Rinse with hot water and dry immediately or dry in the oven with the pilot light on.

Glass and black-finish pans   These are good conductors of heat and brown loaves faster than aluminum. Lower the oven temperature by 25°F when using these pans, as they absorb heat quickly. Glass may be conveniently washed in a dishwasher. The loaf has to be removed immediately from black-finish pans, otherwise the trapped moisture will begin the rust process. Wipe the pan with a clean, dry cloth and store in a dry cupboard. I layer my pans with a section of paper toweling to prevent scratching during storage.

Stainless steel   Durable, easy to clean, and nonreactive to acid foods, but unfortunately, the least efficient conductor of heat. Some bread pans are made from it, but they are not the best choice.

Baking sheets and jelly-roll pans   In addition to loaf pans, square and such rectangular pans as baking sheets and jelly-roll pans are available to the home baker. Look for well-constructed pans of heaviest-gauge aluminum or tin-plated steel. Black steel is fine, but be aware that the finish causes a dark, heavy crust. The sizes of baking sheets range from the classic jelly-roll pan at 10-by-15 inches, with a raised edge of about 1 inch, to the classic all-purpose half-sheet baking sheet at 11-by-16 inches or larger with slightly sloped edges. Baking sheets are also available in air-cushioned and nonstick types. When baking at high oven temperatures, stack 2 baking sheets together—this is called double panning—to slow the temperature and prevent the bottoms of the baked goods from burning.

Sealing clay loaf pans
Clay loaf pans need to be seasoned only before using the first time. Scrub the piece of cookware with liquid detergent and hot water, rinsing thoroughly. Spread a light coating of vegetable oil or spray shortening inside the pan and wipe out the excess with a paper towel. Place the cookware in a 250°F oven for one hour. Remove from the oven and place on a thick pot holder or wire rack to let cool. The cookware is now ready for use.

The Basic Building Blocks: Ingredients

ALWAYS USE GOOD-QUALITY INGREDIENTS IN BREADBAKING. Yeast, flour—whether wheat, rye, or specialty flours—liquid, and salt, as well as sweeteners and fats, all play a role in the final loaf. The following is a guide to their selection and care.

Yeast

I refer to yeast as the soul of bread. It is a one-celled, natural, living plantlike fungus, scientifically known as *Saccharomyces cerevisiae,* that is cultured on vats of molasses. It raises the dough and gives it the characteristic flavor we associate with bread. To be activated and to reproduce, yeast needs the combination of sugar, moisture, warmth, and air. The enzyme action in the yeast converts the sugar and starch in the flour during the rising periods into alcohol—the beerlike or yeasty smell in a raw dough—and carbon dioxide, which becomes trapped within the stretchy meshlike gluten structure of the dough in the process known as rising.

Yeast is sold to the consumer in five different forms: active dry yeast, compressed fresh cake yeast, quick-rise yeast, instant dried yeast, and bread machine yeast. All of the domestic dried yeasts are marketed by the Fleischmann's and Red Star companies. Nutritional yeasts, such as brewer's yeast and torula, are not leavening agents; their yeast cells are dead. When selecting yeast, consider the type of dough you have in mind as a guide to what type of yeast to use. Obviously, use bread machine yeast for that piece of equipment and quick-rise yeast if you like to use the one-step method in an electric mixer. Instant yeast is excellent for bread machines and is best combined with the dry ingredients utilizing the RapidRise method or for overnight retarded refrigerator doughs. Use instant, active dry, or fresh yeast interchangeably in sugar and fat-rich sweet doughs or lean French-style breads and dinner rolls. More yeast is needed if the doughs are rich and sweet than if they are lean since sugar and fat tend to retard the yeast's action, as do embellishments like nuts and dried fruits. Lean doughs can take a very small amount of yeast, but then the fermentation period will be much longer. More yeast may be used to speed up the process with a quick-rise dough, but the flavor will be more yeasty. Always pay attention to the temperature and weather when constructing yeast doughs: Warm, moist weather makes for a faster reacting dough while in cool weather, the process is slowed. Professional bakers adjust for these variables with a cooler or warmer liquid temperature.

ACTIVE DRY YEAST

Active dry yeast is a very stable, dormant form of fresh yeast, popular since the 1940s. It was developed with stability a more important consideration than activity. It is a larger grain size than other dried yeasts. It is sold in dated ¼-ounce packets (three in a strip), 4-ounce jars, in larger quantities by mail order, and in bulk at natural foods stores. One scant tablespoon of dry yeast is equal to a ¼-ounce premeasured package or to a .06-ounce cube of fresh cake yeast. Weight for weight, dry yeast is about twice as potent as compressed fresh, so take care if substituting (see page 131). Dry yeast is not activated until it is dissolved in warm (about 105° to 115°F) liquid. Use an instant-read yeast thermometer to be certain of your liquid temperature until you can tell the exact warmth by feel. Keep dry yeast in the refrigerator in a tightly covered container. Approximately 1 to 2 tablespoons of yeast (about 1 percent of the weight of the flour) are sufficient to rise a dough made with 8 cups of flour. Resist the temptation to add more yeast than called for in a recipe; too much dry yeast makes for a strong, sour flavor. If properly stored, dry yeast can remain active for up to one year. To be certain, always proof your yeast, especially if there are long lapses between baking sprees, and do not buy packages that have exceeded their pull date.

You may find active dry yeast bulk packaged as baker's dry yeast for professional bakeries; it often has a different particle size than the active dry yeast sold at retail. With the large-scale recipe proportions, less yeast is needed to rise a dough. You would use 40 percent as much baker's dry yeast as fresh compressed yeast by weight.

FRESH COMPRESSED CAKE YEAST

Used for centuries, cake yeast is known for its dependability, excellent rising ability, and, some claim, superior flavor compared to dry yeast strains. It is marketed by the Fleischmann's and Red Star companies. Fleischmann, originally an Austrian stillmaster, introduced yeast to America when he set up a baking concession at the Philadelphia Centennial Exposition in 1876. He baked fresh bread with his now famous Culture #40 on the premises, enticing the masses with the aroma. Fresh yeast is the favorite of American and European artisanal bakers, known for their practices of lower temperatures and slower proofing techniques. Increasingly difficult to find, it is sold in .06-ounce cubes, 2-ounce cakes in natural food stores in the refrigerated section, and 1-pound blocks, sometimes available to home bakers from local bakeries. The 1-pound professional size is absolutely the best fresh yeast for the dedicated baker and I highly recommend it if you can find it. To prolong shelf life, the smaller cakes sold in the supermarket are stabilized with starch, which tends to slightly decrease their overall potency. When fresh, it is an even tan-gray to light yellow-brown color with no discoloration and it breaks with a clean edge. Compressed yeast should be dissolved in tepid liquids (about 80° to 95°F) before being added to the dry ingredients in a recipe. The difference between fresh and dry yeast lies in moisture content only, not rising powers. Fresh compressed yeast is highly perishable; it must be refrigerated at about 30°F, and it will keep for about 2 weeks before molding. Compressed yeast may be successfully frozen for several months, but its potency seems to decrease.

QUICK-RISE YEAST

Quick-rise yeast was developed in 1984 in response to the large amount of home baking being done by new, more powerful home mixers. It is a new strain of low-moisture active dry yeast, which is fed with larger amounts of phosphorus and ammonia to increase the enzyme activity and contains conditioners, in the form of emulsifiers and antioxidants, that raise dough activity 50 percent faster than regular active dry yeast. The particle size, finer than that of active dry yeast, works best when added directly to the dry ingredients, without prior rehydration, and with the liquid at about 120° to 125°F when added. Follow the manufacturer's instructions, since dough temperature and rising times are different than for general bread making. I find there is a small loss of flavor and keeping quality in the finished loaves, because of the yeast's fast fermentation, so I avoid using it when other yeast is available, but it is totally interchangeable with other dry yeasts if necessary. Use a bit less quick-rise yeast in a recipe where a slower, more normal rising time is desired. It is available in ¼-ounce packages, sold in a 3-package strip, and in 4-ounce jars. Keep quick-rise yeast in the refrigerator in a tightly covered container.

INSTANT DRIED YEAST

Instant dried yeast is the latest development in yeast science. It was originally created in the late 1960s and is imported from the European S.I. Lasaffre Company, SAF, which is the oldest yeast manufacturer in France. The yeast is carefully dried in small batches to a very low percentage of moisture, yet it has properties that make it as active as compressed fresh yeast since there are no excess dead cells as in active dry yeast. It has rod-shaped free-flowing granules that are developed with easy measuring in mind. Since this instant yeast has three times as many yeast cells as active dry yeast, you can use up to 25 percent less instant yeast and one-third the amount of fresh cake yeast. Use only a bit less in converting a recipe using quick-rise yeast. A different strain of yeast cells than our domestic brands, Regular Instant, an all-purpose yeast with a red packaging label, is coated with a layer of dead yeast cells and is quite perishable once the vacuum package is opened. This strain of instant yeast cannot tolerate a lot of sugar, as in sweet dough recipes, or long, slow proofing temperatures, because it is constantly rising. Special Instant, with the gold label, is coated with ascorbic acid and a form of sugar, which enables the yeast to activate immediately on contact with warm liquid, in contrast to domestic dry yeast, which needs some sugar or starch to activate properly. This strain is sugar-tolerant for use in sweet doughs and for use in long-rise yeast-fortified sponges. Instant yeast enables a dough to be baked without any initial fermentation period. Once the vacuum package is opened, instant yeast must be stored in the freezer. It can be frozen for up to 1 year.

BREAD MACHINE YEAST

Bread machine yeast, the latest member of the yeast family, was developed to meet the increased demand of electronically-oriented home bakers. It is finely granulated and coated with ascorbic acid and a flour buffer to make it stable enough to be mixed directly with the flour and other dry ingredients before the liquid is added and to be not as sensitive as active dry yeast to temperature changes. With care, it may be used interchangeably with active dry yeast and quick-rise yeast.

SUBSTITUTING FRESH YEAST FOR DRY YEAST AND VICE VERSA

Fresh compressed yeast and granular active dry yeasts may be used interchangeably in recipes.

- One .06-ounce cube of fresh compressed yeast is equivalent to one ¼-ounce package, a scant tablespoon, of active dry yeast.
- One .06-ounce cube of fresh compressed yeast is equivalent to 2¼ teaspoons of instant yeast.
- One 2-ounce cake of fresh compressed yeast is equivalent to a scant 1 ounce of active dry yeast, 3½ packages, or about 3 tablespoons.
- One ¼-ounce package of active dry yeast, a scant tablespoon, is equivalent to 2 teaspoons of instant yeast.
- One ¼-ounce package of quick-rise yeast, a scant tablespoon, is equivalent to 2¼ teaspoons of instant yeast.
- One pound of fresh compressed yeast is equivalent to 7½ to 8 ounces of active dry or other granular dry yeast.

Flour

Because the type of flour used in a recipe is the major ingredient and the foundation for all baking, it will determine the nature of the loaf. Wheat flour is composed of moisture, which varies with the climatic conditions and storage before milling; protein (gluten-forming qualities), which varies with different types of wheat; starch granules, which make up 75 percent of the flour and are necessary for texture; fat, which is present in the wheat germ and can easily turn rancid; enzymes, which are converted into simple sugars that are food for the yeast and facilitate browning; and mineral ash, which is present in the bran. Brands of flour vary in the amount of liquid they absorb, but all yeast breads require some wheat flour for proper structure. Learn to recognize different kinds of flours by sight and by feel: Unbleached bread flour and all-purpose flour are creamy white and slightly coarse to the touch; cake flour is very smooth, fine, and pure white; pastry flour is more creamy, like bread flour, yet is smooth and fine textured. Organic stone-ground whole wheat flour is coarse and gritty; finely ground whole wheat flour is quite smooth and pale brown in color. Other earthy specialty flours, such as rye, corn, oat, and buckwheat, are easily mixed in small proportions with wheat flour for nutritious, flavorful loaves.

THE WHEAT FAMILY

Wheat comes in hard and soft varieties. Special kinds of hard wheat include spelt, known as the bread wheats; kamut; and durum, known as the pasta wheat. By-products of milling white flours are unprocessed bran and the wheat germ, which add color, nutrition, and fiber to breads.

UNBLEACHED BREAD FLOUR, ALSO CALLED HIGH-GLUTEN FLOUR: Made from hard red spring wheat that is aged without chemicals or preservatives for the best results. Cream-colored, it has a protein content of 12 to 14 percent. High-gluten wheat absorbs more liquid than other flours, creating a more elastic dough and light-textured bread.

UNBLEACHED ALL-PURPOSE FLOUR: Blended from several wheats to an approximate combination of 80 percent hard wheat and 20 percent soft. It is perfectly good for bread. Brands of unbleached flour vary in protein or gluten content from place to place. Unbleached flour sold in the southern states has a higher percentage of soft wheat; that sold in northern, midwestern, and western states contains a higher percentage of hard wheat. Unbleached flour is aged naturally to oxidize the proteins and bleach out the natural yellow pigment present in freshly milled flour (also known as green flour). Bleached flour is aged quickly with chlorine dioxide.

CAKE FLOUR, WHITE PASTRY FLOUR, OR INSTANT FLOUR (LIKE WONDRA): These are not suitable for baking breads. The exception is whole wheat pastry flour, which makes wonderful bread. These flours contain only about 8 percent protein and are milled very fine. Save them for biscuits, muffins, cakes, and pastries.

SELF-RISING FLOUR: This contains leavening in the form of bicarbonate of soda, and salt. It cannot be used for yeast breads and should not be substituted for cake flour.

WHOLE WHEAT AND GRAHAM FLOURS: These are ground from the whole wheat berry, including the oil-rich bran and germ. They have an intensely nutty flavor and come in a variety of textures from fine to coarse, and bake up into chewy-crusted breads. They contain less gluten than white flours and work differently in yeast breads than white flour.

WHITE WHOLE WHEAT: A new strain of winter wheat from Kansas that is especially sweet and light colored. It may be substituted for regular whole wheat flour.

SEMOLINA FLOUR: The finely ground endosperm of durum wheat, yellow in color, is used extensively in pasta making. It makes a delicious, high-protein addition to Italian-style breads. Semolina flour is not the same as semolina meal, which is a coarsely ground wheat cereal like farina, ground from the endosperm only, or Wheateena, ground whole grain wheat. Semolina meal is used in a manner similar to coarse cornmeal.

SPELT: An ancient strain of wheat that has less protein than regular whole wheats, but it has its own unique flavor. Spelt may be substituted for regular whole wheat flour.

KAMUT: A Montana wheat developed from another ancient strain of wheat with an oat-sweet aroma.

CRACKED WHEAT: A fine, medium, or coarse cut of the wheat kernel.

BULGUR WHEAT: Parboiled and dried cracked wheat.

MIXED GRAIN CEREALS AND WHEAT BLEND MEALS: Very popular in breads, these add texture, flavor, and fiber: Roman Meal, Wheateena, Quaker Multi-Grain Cereal, Cream of Wheat (farina), Muesli, and six-, eight-, nine-, and ten-grain blends that consist of wheat, rye, barley, triticale, corn, oats, flax, millet, brown rice, wheat germ, wheat bran, and soy grits in varying proportions. King Arthur Flour Baker's Catalog offers unique German cereal blends for bread baking, such as Multikorn Mix and Jogging Brot Mix, which combine crushed grains, seeds, nuts, and dried fruit to be mixed into the dough.

Specialty Flours

BARLEY: Barley has a chewy texture and a mild, sweet flavor. Hulled pearl barley can be toasted and rolled into flakes, which are used like rolled oats, or ground into a low-gluten flour with a grayish color. Tannish barley flour is ground from barley meal. Barley malt, a sweet syrup made from the toasted and dried whole grain, is similar to molasses; it's a wonderful sweetener for breads.

BUCKWHEAT: Buckwheat is technically not a grain, but the seed of a red-stemmed herb plant related to rhubarb. Buckwheat flour, ground from its triangular groat known as kasha, is low in protein, which makes for a tender baked product with an assertive, slightly bitter flavor and a purple-gray color. The buckwheat grown in Europe has a rather mild taste, distinctly different from the Japanese buckwheat grown in the United States, which can be quite earthy. A pale, mild-flavored silverskin buckwheat is grown in northern Maine (available from Bouchard Family Farm, 1-800-239-3237). Small amounts of buckwheat flour combined with wheat flour make a good light-textured bread.

CHESTNUT: New to American breadmakers, chestnut flour is ground from dried chestnuts. The flavor varies with how the nuts have been peeled. The flour's beige texture is dust-fine and the flavor distinctive.

CORN: Yellow cornmeal comes in several grinds, from fine to coarse, which are used for making sweet yeasted cornbreads. Degerminated cornmeal has had the germ removed for longer shelf life. Search out coarse yellow polenta, or corn grits. Masa harina is finely ground cornmeal made from lime-treated hominy; it is used for making tortillas. Baked goods made with cornmeal are crumbly in texture and a bit gritty, with a characteristic pale yellow color. Cornmeal is unique in flavor and texture—there is no substitute for it. Stone-ground cornmeal is preferable, with the germ intact; it should be labeled nondegerminated. Store stone-ground cornmeal in the refrigerator; it can go rancid quickly at room temperature. Blue, white, or masa cornmeals may be substituted for the yellow cornmeal in breads.

MILLET: Tiny round yellow grains of millet resemble pale mustard seeds. Millet has a mild slightly nutty taste and a fluffy texture, and it is very easy to digest. Use the whole millet seed or cracked millet grits as a "crunchy munchy" addition to other grains and seeds in a dough that bakes up into a firm, chewy bread.

OATS: Rolled oats are the most familiar breakfast cereal on the market. Whole groats are hulled, steamed, and flattened into old-fashioned flakes. When rerolled they become quick-cooking oats. Quick and old-fashioned oats can be used interchangeably. They may be ground into oat flour with a food processor for a coarse meal suitable for bread making. The mild, nutty flavor and moist, nubby texture of oats is a favorite in breads.

RICE: There are thousands of varieties of rice, each with its own distinct flavor, texture, aroma, and color. Rice flour may be ground from brown or white rice, although I always use brown rice flour. It is an excellent thickener and is good for dusting, as it absorbs moisture slowly. It has a light, sweet flavor (use it in working with pizza and focaccia doughs). Rice flour is a favorite in nongluten diets. Avoid sweet rice flour; it is not suitable for baking breads.

RYE: Rye has a characteristically bitter-strong, earthy flavor and contains a small amount of gluten. It is popular in Scandinavian and Eastern European breads. Whole-grain rye, known as the groat or berry, is ground into light rye flour, also known as cream of rye; it is great for all-purpose dusting of loaves as it is nearly white in color. Medium rye is the easiest to find in supermarkets. Dark rye has varying proportions of bran, with pumpernickel flour the coarsest of all. Rolled rye flakes are similar to oatmeal and cracked rye, all of which need soaking or cooking before use and are also good additions in breads.

HOME GRIST MILLS OR KITCHEN GRAIN MILLS

Many baking aficionados swear by freshly milled flour, the kind you grind yourself, as the finest flavor available. Home mills are hand- or motor-powered, equipped with stone or steel plates that rotate on the stationary milling surface to crush or cut the grain. This is purely a matter of personal taste; owning and operating a home grain mill is an investment in time and money. Since whole-grain flours go rancid, B vitamins in the germ begin to oxidize as soon as the freshly milled flour is exposed to air, and commercial milling is often done under high temperatures, home milling has some advantages. There is a minimal time lapse between milling the grain and mixing the dough. Also, you can buy the whole grains, from wheat and rye to amaranth and barley, and grind them in different textures, depending on your needs. There is a practical model for every bread baker's taste and aesthetics: The heavy, rustic cast-stone Samap hand mill is the link to the ancient household stone querns; the counter-clamped steel Corona hand mill for masa and cracked grains; the incredibly efficient plastic-bodied electric mills designed to grind hard wheat berries and corn kernels as fine or as coarse as you want; the Canadian Kootenay model, set with natural quarried stones in a wooden housing to resemble a miniature water-powered wheel mill; and finally, the grinding attachment for the KitchenAid mixer.

Liquids

Water is the most important liquid in forming a dough. It binds the flour and yeast and determines the consistency of the dough by swelling the strands of gluten. The ratio of flour to water is about 3 to 1. Be certain to use bottled or spring water; municipal sources and deep wells often contain minerals and foreign matter that affect fermentation. Milk, buttermilk, yogurt, sour cream, potato cooking water, fruit and vegetable juices, beer, wine, and coconut milk may all be used as the liquid in recipes, adding food value and flavor, as well as extending shelf life. Liquids are best used when warm, in the range of 100° to 120°F, to activate the yeast properly. An instant-read thermometer is invaluable for this task. Each recipe specifies the ideal liquid temperature. One cup of liquid absorbs approximately 3 to 4 cups of flour to form a dough.

Sweeteners

❋

Granulated sugar, brown sugar, honey, maple products, molasses, barley malt, and fruit purées add flavor and serve as a food for the yeast, but they are not essential ingredients. However, they prolong freshness by retaining moisture, and they produce a distinctive golden to dark brown crust. One tablespoon of sweetener for every 2 cups of flour is the average addition to a standard loaf bread, but many sweet loaves contain much higher amounts. Large amounts of sugar in a dough cause it to rise more slowly since they weaken the gluten structure, so plan accordingly.

Fats

❋

Butter and oils contribute a fine, tender texture and a rich flavor. Many breads, such as French and Italian loaves, contain none; these are known as lean doughs. Fats also prolong freshness by retaining moisture and by lubricating the gluten mesh network so it can expand with little effort. One teaspoon of fat for every 2 cups of flour is the average minimum addition to standard loaf breads.

Salt

❋

Salt is used as a flavor and aroma enhancer. I use a fine-grind of sea salt exclusively; it has no preservatives, but it does have its own special flavor. It also whitens the crumb. It slightly retards the action of the yeast and strengthens the gluten, making it more stretchy, thus contributing to a loaf's finished texture. Since salt also inhibits the growth of yeast, it is also used to control fermentation and the growth of ever-present air-borne wild yeasts. The general amount of salt is 1 to 1½ teaspoons for every 3½ cups, or 1 pound, of flour. If using coarse salt crystals, grind them fine in a hand salt mill or save them for sprinkling.

The Bread Baker's Pantry

STOCKING A KITCHEN IS AN ART IN ITSELF, AND YOUR baking will be marked by your individual style. The following pantry list for the home bread baker is based on my own. A well-stocked pantry is a precious time-saver—if a pantry is stocked with the basics of flour, salt, and dry yeast—crusty, golden homemade loaves of unparalleled freshness are only a few hours away. They are your building blocks, and the end product will only be as good as the ingredients you use to construct them. Expand your horizons by using specialty flours, such as buckwheat, rye, graham, and blue cornmeal. You'll want a few dried herbs, pure extracts, some liqueurs, dried fruits, and flavorful oils on hand, too. The culinary calendar turns up surprises throughout the year, such as fresh-picked berries or apples and pears, which will enhance your basic doughs.

Invest in a variety of good-quality plastic containers with tight-fitting lids for storage. Unbleached flour keeps for up to a year at room temperature in an airtight container to avoid sweating (the absorption of moisture from the air), but whole-grain flours *must* be refrigerated or frozen to retain freshness, especially buckwheat, cornmeal, and chestnut flours. Label for easy identification; flours can resemble each other. Store yeast in the refrigerator for maximum shelf life. Dried fruits, nuts, and herbs may be frozen in freezer storage bags. I store sesame and poppy seeds in the freezer because they are used in small quantities over a long period of time and the aromatic oils go rancid, as they do with nuts. To preserve the bounty of seasons past, I keep homemade candied lemon and orange peels and dried fruits in the freezer; they keep perfectly for up to a year. Persimmon and winter squash purées keep well in freezer containers, as does extra cooked rice. I refrigerate extracts, cold-pressed oils (except for olive oil, which will congeal), and maple syrup.

When shopping, take into account your own preferences, but do not overbuy perishables; dairy and whole-grain flours, for example, are best fresh. And don't forget to put away a good selection of your favorite jams, jellies, fruit curds, and preserves to showcase thick slices of warm, homemade bread for breakfast toast or a snack. Piquant chutneys and Dijon and coarse-grained mustards are a must with sweet butter and homemade lemon mayonnaise for memorable sandwiches. Prepare a traditional *smørrebrød*, the Danish open-faced sandwich luncheon, using your firm-textured fresh rye, wheat, and white breads. The elaborate Swedish *smörgåsbord* or Russian *zakuski* bread and butter tables are a good place to highlight your homemade breads—

loaves, freeform, or flat and stuffed breads. Spreadable cheeses go perfectly with a basket of crusty rolls, making a bevy of simple ingredients into a satisfying and often dramatic combination of foods.

    If you are one of those busy bakers who find the time-consuming ritual of baking reserved for weekends and vacations, keep your freezer stocked with extra loaves of homemade bread, ready to be defrosted and reheated, or popped into the toaster at a moment's notice.

Dry Goods

❀

Confections
Australian candied ginger
Australian glacéed whole fruits
Homemade candied orange and lemon peels
Homemade honey-glazed dried fruits
Italian whole candied chestnuts

Dairy
Nonfat dry milk, dry buttermilk, dry goat's milk
    powder

Dried fruits and vegetables
Apples
Apricots
Cherries
Cranberries
Currants
Dates
Figs
Pears
Pineapple
Prunes
Raisins, dark and golden
Tomatoes

Flavorings
Carob powder
Chocolate, unsweetened and semisweet
Cocoa, unsweetened Dutch process
Instant espresso powder

Flour and grains
Wheat flour
    High-gluten bread flour
    Unbleached all-purpose flour
Whole wheat flour, stone-ground, coarse and fine
    grinds
    Graham flour
    White whole wheat flour
    Whole wheat pastry flour
Semolina flour or durum flour
Cracked wheat and whole wheat berries
Rye flour, fine, medium, and pumpernickel grinds

❀

Specialty flours and grains

Barley and barley flour

Buckwheat

Chestnut flours

Cornmeal, coarse and fine grinds, yellow, white,
   blue, polenta, and masa harina

Millet, seed and grits

Oats, Irish oatmeal, old-fashioned rolled and quick-
   cooking, and steel-cut oats

Seven-grain cereal

White and brown rice

Wild rice

Herbs and spices

Allspice, cinnamon, cloves, and mace, ground

Basil, dill, marjoram, oregano, rosemary, tarragon,
   dried or frozen

Cardamom, ground and pods

Garlic, onions, and shallots

Hungarian paprika, sweet *rósza* and half-sweet *félédes*

New Mexican red chile powder and chili powder
   mixture

Nutmeg and black peppercorns, whole

Nuts

Almonds

Chestnuts, fresh or frozen steam-peeled

Hazelnuts

Pecans

Pine nuts

Pistachios

Walnuts

Salt

Sea salt or iodized, fine and coarse grinds

Seeds

Anise

Caraway

Fennel

Nigella, also called black caraway

Poppy

Pumpkin

Sesame

Sunflower

Sugar and sweeteners

Dried barley malt extract powder

Granulated maple sugar

Granulated white sugar

Light brown sugar

Powdered or confectioners' sugar

Sucanat

Yeast

Active dry yeast

Wet Goods

❋

Eggs

Egg replacer

Large white or brown eggs

Flavorings and extracts

Extracts: almond, anise, coconut, lemon, orange,
  and vanilla

Almond paste

Chestnut purée, sweetened

Vinegar: balsamic, fruit, and sherry

Liquid sweeteners

Barley malt syrup

Corn syrup, light and dark

Golden syrup, imported

Honey, local and imported

Maple syrup

Molasses, light or dark

Milk and milk products

Buttermilk

Cottage cheese/ricotta cheese

Crème fraîche

Goat's milk

Milk, whole, low-fat, or nonfat

Sour cream, regular and low-fat

Yogurt

Oils and Butter

Butter, unsalted

Margarine

Olive oil, different grades

Nut oils: almond, hazelnut, sunflower, and walnut

Vegetable oils: canola, safflower, or flavorless
  blends

Other special ingredients

Applesauce, unsweetened

Brandy, liqueurs (especially nut and orange), and
  wines (especially mead and apricot)

Concentrated fruit syrups

Normandy hard cider, beer

Olives and capers

❋

Mail-Order Sources

THE FOLLOWING SOURCES CAN SUPPLY all the flours and grains required for baking with this book. The King Arthur catalog is also good for all equipment (they carry the hard-to-find 8½-by-4¾-inch stoneware loaf pans) and the Penzey's spice catalog is one of the best in the country. Chukar Cherries carries dried blueberries and cranberries as well as cherries, and Gray's Mill is famous for its stone-ground cornmeal.

West Coast
Chukar Cherries
306 Wine Country Road
Prosser, WA 99350
1-800-624-9544

Pamela's Products Inc./Giustos
156 Utah Avenue
South San Francisco, CA 94080
1-415-952-4546

Central States
Arrowhead Mills, Inc.
P.O. Box 2059
Hereford, TX 79045
1-806-364-0730

Penzey's, Ltd. Spice House
P. O. Box 1448
Waukesha, WI 53187
1-414-574-0277

East Coast
Gray's Grist Mill
P.O. Box 422
Adamsville, RI 02801
1-508-636-6075

King Arthur Flour Baker's Catalog
P.O. Box 876
Norwich, VT 05055
1-800-827-6836

High-Altitude Guide

ALTITUDES OVER 3,000 FEET AFFECT BAKING PROCEDURES. The atmosphere is drier, due to lower air pressure, and flours dry out; bread recipes require slightly more liquid to produce a soft, silky yeast dough. Water usually takes longer to boil. Sugar and chocolate tend to become more concentrated in batters, and liquid evaporates quickly. The scientist in you will need to closely observe results and experiment to get the proper dough consistencies for your yeast breads. Asking a neighbor or coworker for first-hand information is the best way to go. There are also special reference books devoted to the art of high-altitude baking for people who live at altitudes higher than 3,000 feet.

Fermentation and rising is faster the higher you go as the leavening carbon dioxide gases are able to expand faster due to the thinner air, and rising times will be decreased up to one half. Overrising causes a finished loaf to be coarse in texture. For bread baking there is really only one technique to remember: *To avoid overrising, reduce yeast by ½ teaspoon for every tablespoon or package called for in the recipe.* A second rise to just nearly double in bulk is recommended for the best flavor and texture. No temperature adjustment of liquids is necessary.

Oven Temperature   Increase by 25°F to compensate for faster rising in the oven and slower heating. The same rules apply to sourdough and quick-bread baking.

Liquids   For each cup, increase the amount by 1 tablespoon at more than 3,000 feet; 2 to 3 tablespoons at 5,000 feet; and 3 to 4 tablespoons at 7,000 to 8,000 feet.

Sugar   For each cup, decrease the amount by 1 tablespoon at more than 3,000 feet; 2 tablespoons at 5,000 feet; and 3 tablespoons at 7,000 to 8,000 feet.

Flour   For each cup, increase flour by 1 tablespoon at more than 3,000 feet; 2 tablespoons at 5,000 feet; and 3 tablespoons at more than 6,500 feet. Store flour in airtight containers.

Kitchen Weights, Measures, and Metrics

HOUSEHOLD BREAD RECIPES MADE BY OUR GRANNIES are notorious for their lack of consistent measure: a pinch of common sense in place of a cup, instinct instead of a thermometer, and experience instead of a timer were commonplace baking skills. The bread was, in most cases, beautiful and tasty, even without standard measuring tools and a recognizable balanced formula. These recipes are the basis for many of the fine breads being made today and have been written down so that contemporary bakers can make the same recipe with little variation. Luckily, a bread recipe can vary slightly in measurement and still produce a wonderful loaf, with domestic kitchen scales often as imprecise as the baker's haphazard dip and sweep.

Taking bread baking out of the realm of the romantic and artistic into the scientific, I have included here my reference table for converting some common solid and liquid exact measures to their metric equivalents. The process of measuring dry weight by scaling is an ancient practice, balancing quantities against standard and constant weights.

You will find this chart especially useful when translating European or large-quantity bread recipes for use in your home kitchen. Many bread recipes are now conveniently written for both U.S. and metric values, since legions of trained bakers have been taught to measure all their ingredients by weight. It is a system commonly employed in restaurant and professional kitchens, so that results are as consistent and reliable as possible. I have pored over countless tables of conversions to compile a chart simple enough to use regularly in my own baking forays.

The U.S. standard of measures for dry and liquid capacities are the tablespoon, cup, pint, and quart. The British imperial system is the old method of pounds, ounces, and gills used throughout the British Empire. I visualize them as king-sized U.S. liquid measures and scant dry cup measures, since much of the language is the same. This system has slowly been replaced in the last twenty years with the metric system, used throughout the world now, except in the United States and Belize, with grams for dry measure and liters for liquid measure, calculated in convenient units of ten. Larger and smaller units are calculated by multiplying or dividing by 10, 100, or 1,000. Please note the liquid gram is the same quantity as the milliliter, both having one thousand units each, which can be confusing to the uninitiated when called for in recipes.

For the most consistent baking results, equip your kitchen with a baker's balance scale, electronic, or spring scale that registers both U.S. and metric weight, with measuring cups for liquids, and measuring spoons and cups for dry ingredients. Dry cup measures afford the most accurate measuring of flour because you can scrape the top. Bread making does not suffer from a slight variation in cup measurement or unaerated flour, although pastry making does. When weighing, measure flour into a small paper or plastic bag set into the scale's measuring bowl for the least mess. To become accustomed to the terms, note the following:

- A kilogram (a measure of weight) is slightly more than 2 pounds.
- A gram is about 1/30 ounce and a heaping ½ teaspoon of flour weighs about 1 gram.
- A liter (a measure of volume) is slightly more than a quart.
- A deciliter is slightly less than ½ cup and a centiliter is about 2 teaspoons.
- A meter (a measure of length) is slightly more than 3 feet.
- A decimeter is slightly less than 4 inches and a centimeter about ⅜ inch.
- Temperature is regulated to units of degree Celsius with 100°C the boiling point of water and 0°C the freezing point.
- One degree Celsius is equivalent to about 2°F.
- One pint of water weighs about 1 pound in U.S. measure.

The following standard loaf recipe is written for both U.S. and metric measurements so you can see how a recipe looks when written for both systems. I find this very helpful when translating European recipes.

Metric	Ingredients	U.S.
700–830 g	Unsifted all-purpose flour	5½ to 6½ cups
36 g	Sugar	3 tablespoons
12 g	Salt	2 teaspoons
7 g	Active dry yeast	Scant 1 tablespoon
240 ml	Water	1 cup
240 ml	Milk	1 cup
45 g	Butter	3 tablespoons

Two 22-by-12.5-by-6.5 cm (8½-by-4½-by-2½ inch) loaf pans

Flour

Unsifted, Unbleached All-Purpose, Bread, and
  Light Whole Wheat

Spoons/Cups	Ounces/Pounds	Grams/Kilograms
½ cup	2½ oz	70 g
1 cup	4¾ oz	140 g
3½ cups	1 lb	450 g
About 7 cups	2 lb	900 g
About 18 cups	5 lb	2.25 kg
½ cup cake flour	2¼ oz	60 g
2 cups cake flour	8½ oz	240 g

Sugar

Spoons/Cups	Ounces/Pounds	Grams
2 Tbs granulated	1 oz	30 g
½ cup granulated	3½ oz	100 g
1 cup granulated	7 oz	200 g
2¼ cups granulated	1 lb	450 g
½ cup brown sugar	2⅔ oz	80 g
1 cup brown sugar	5⅓ oz	160 g
1 cup powdered	4¼ oz	140 g
3⅓ cups powdered	1 lb	450 g

Butter

Spoons/Cups	Ounces/Pounds	Grams
2 Tbs	1 oz (¼ stick)	30 g
½ cup	4 oz (1 stick)	125 g
1 cup	½ lb (2 sticks)	225 g
2 cups	1 lb (4 sticks)	450 g

Chocolate

Squares/Cups	Ounces	Grams
1 square unsweetened	1 oz	30 g
1 cup semisweet chips	6 oz	175 g
1 cup unsweetened cocoa	4 oz	115 g

Eggs

Number	Spoons/Cups
1 large whole egg (2 oz)	3 Tbs
5 large whole eggs	1 cup
8 large egg whites	1 cup
12 large egg yolks	1 cup

Dried fruits and nuts

Cups	Ounces/Pounds	Grams
Almonds (whole shelled, blanched, slivered)		
¾ cup	4 oz	120 g
3 cups	1 lb	450 g
Pecans (halves)		
4 cups	1 lb	450 g
Walnuts (halves, chopped)		
3½ cups	1 lb	450 g
Seedless raisins		
1 cup	5¼ oz	160 g
3 cups	1 lb	450 g

Liquids

Water, Milk, Buttermilk, Cream, Wine, Spirits, Juice

Spoons / Cups	Ounces / Pounds	Grams / Kilograms Milliliters / Liters
1 Tb	½ oz	15 g/ml
¼ cup	2 oz	60 g/ml
1 cup	8 oz	225 g/ml
2 cups	1 lb	450 g/45 cl
4 cups	32 oz	900 g/90 cl
4¼ cups	36 oz	1 kg/1 l

Inches to Centimeters

⅜ in	1 cm
1 in	2.5 cm
1½ in	4 cm
3 in	7.5 cm
6 in	15.5 cm
8 in	20 cm
9½ in	24 cm
10 in	25.5 cm
12 in	30 cm

ounce	=	oz
pound	=	lb
milliliter	=	ml
centiliter	=	cl
liter	=	l
gram	=	g
kilogram	=	kg
inch	=	inch
centimeter	=	cm

Bread Lexicon

A REFERENCE GUIDE TO THE TERMS USED IN THIS COLLECTION of recipes, including ingredients, equipment, techniques, European vocabulary, and details on the understanding of the parts of wheat and the properties of flour.

Absorption The ability of ground or cracked grains to absorb moisture to produce the desired consistency needed to make a dough ball.

Aleurone The aleurone and the pericarp layers that compose the outer covering of the wheat berry commonly known as bran.

All-purpose flour A mixture of hard and soft wheats, 80 and 20 percent respectively, for all-round baking purposes.

Baguette A French national symbol, the old-fashioned, authentic rod-like slender white flour loaf with a crisp crust. About 3 inches in diameter and up to 32 inches long, weighing about 8 ounces, it is made with only wheat flour, water, yeast, and salt.

Baking off A professional term for the period that the bread is baking in the dry heat of the oven.

Bannetons Woven wicker basket molds in a variety of sizes, lined with unbleached linen or muslin and seasoned with flour to prevent sticking, in which to rise bread doughs before baking.

Barley malt syrup A thick, concentrated sweet syrup extracted from sprouted barley. Used as a substitute for molasses or honey in breads.

Beat Technique to rapidly whip air into a batter and change it into a smooth consistency with a combination of stirring and mixing.

Bench A professional term for the baker's work table or surface.

Berry Term to describe a whole grain minus its loose hull.

Biga A dough sponge starter of flour, water, and yeast. Known as a "poolish" in France.

Blé French word for wheat.

Bleached flour Wheat flour that's been turned pure white by a chemical process using chlorine dioxide gas to speed up the natural aging process and develop the proteins.

Blend Technique combining two or more ingredients together with a horizontal stirring motion by hand or machine until the mixture is smooth and uniform.

Boulangerie French bread bakery.

Brioche Derived from the French words *bris* (break) and *hocher* (stir). A popular yeasted French cakebread made in many degrees of richness, with a princely brioche containing a high proportion of butter and eggs to flour and a common brioche a low one.

Caramelize To cook sugar over high heat until it becomes a syrupy golden brown liquid.

Cocoa The dry powder remaining after the fatty cocoa butter is extracted out of blocks of unsweetened chocolate liquor.

Combine To mix two or more ingredients together until evenly blended.

Cream To combine fat and sugar or flour to evenly distribute the ingredients and incorporate air.

Dissolve To change a solid into a liquid.

Double panning Setting a baking sheet on top of another of the same size to protect the bottom of the dough from burning in a high-temperature oven.

Dough A thick uncooked mixture primarily of flour and liquid combined with a leavener. The elementary source for creating bread.

Dusting A light spray. Dusting may be done with a ground spice, flour, semolina, farina, or cornmeal. Professionals swear by using light rye flour on the bench during forming.

Endosperm The starchy portion of the wheat berry, which is ground into flour.

Farine French word for flour.

Fermentation The chemical interaction between yeast and carbohydrates that form alcohol and carbon dioxide, which causes the dough to expand.

Fiber The roughage or bulk of a grain plant. It may be insoluble or soluble. Unbleached flour contains 75 percent as much fiber contained in whole wheat flour.

Flour Milled grain.

Frangipane A rich almond cream used as a filling in various yeasted dessert pastries and breads.

Germ The embryo of the wheat berry containing enzymes, proteins, and high concentrations of vitamins B and E.

Glaze A small amount of wet ingredients or beaten egg to brush over the surface of baked and unbaked goods to produce a thin, shiny coat and a finished appearance. Also known as dorure, or gilding, in France.

Gluten The proteins in wheat flour, gliadin and glutenin, that becomes stretchy when kneaded or beaten.

Grainy Rough- or harsh-textured.

Greasing Applying fat to a surface to prevent sticking during baking.

Grits Coarsely cracked grains.

Hard wheat Produces flour high in protein (10 to 13 percent) used especially for bread.

Hearth bread Bread baked directly on the floor of the oven, often lined with earthenware tiles, rather than in a mold.

Humidity The water content of the air.

Instant-read thermometer A thermometer that contains a dial on one end and a point at the other for insertion into a slurry, dough, or baked bread to determine the exact temperature.

Knead From the Anglo-Saxon Old English word *cnotta*, meaning "to knot." An important step in making yeast bread doughs, kneading manipulates a mass of dough to develop the gluten and evenly distribute the yeast molecules.

Kugelhopf pan An intricately fluted tube pan used for making rich sweet yeast breads, in comparison to bundt pans, which are simplier and have curved portions, and a ring mold, which has no flute definition.

Lekvar A thick cooked fruit and sugar filling or spread made with prunes or apricots. A Hungarian specialty.

Levure French word for yeast.

Loaf pan The traditional rectangular shaped tin or ceramic mold to form sandwich breads.

Meal A very coarse grind of any grain, which adds texture to doughs.

Measure To determine the exact amount of liquid and dry ingredients.

Mix Technique combining two or more ingredients with a circular cutting motion into the batter until well integrated.

Molasses A sweet, dark-colored, heavy syrup made from sugar cane.

Molding A professional term for forming the shape of a loaf or rolls.

Nut A dry fruit consisting of an edible kernel enclosed in a dry shell. Nuts may be used whole, chopped, or ground in breads and fillings. From the Old English word *hnutu*.

Oreille Literally the ear or slit in the crust caused by the expansion of the dough when it comes in contact with the heat of the oven, usually on the side of a loaf.

Oven spring The final rise and setting of the cells in yeast bread when the dough comes in contact with the high heat of the oven.

Pane integrale Italian whole wheat bread.

Pane francese Italian French bread.

Pasta sfogliata Italian puff pastry.

Pearl sugar White sugar that has been processed into round grains about six times larger than granulated sugar to be used as a decorative garnish rather than an ingredient.

Pecan The rich, buttery flavored *pakan* is the Algonquin Indian name for "tough nut to crack," native to the American Southeast.

Peel Long-handled flat shovel to place and remove breads from a hearth oven.

Pétrissage French word for kneading.

Pistolets Another French term for *petits pains* (small breads).

Pointage The French term describing the first rising of the dough in a smooth mass after the initial kneading and before deflating and shaping.

Polish The term used for removing the hull of a whole grain and a flour that retains flecks of bran.

Poolish The French dough sponge starter of flour, water, and yeast.

Powdered sugar Also known as confectioners' sugar. White sugar is powdered to give it the ability to dissolve instantly and is then blended with a bit of cornstarch to prevent lumping, making it perfect for glazing and dusting, but not an ingredient to be used in doughs.

Proof A professional term for the period of resting time allowed for a yeast slurry, sponge starter, or dough to rise.

Remonce A pastry filling of creamed butter, sugar, vanilla, and spice widely used in Denmark for Danish pastry.

Retarded dough Dough with fermentation slowed by refrigeration.

Rich dough A yeast dough with high proportions of fat, sugar, or eggs.

Rising Also referred to as the fermentation period. Rising is the time given to allow the yeast to multiply and release carbon dioxide bubbles, which cause the dough to swell.

Rolled-in dough A yeast dough technique in which fat is incorporated in distinct layers by folding and rolling for steam separation during baking, creating a multilayered effect.

Rolling The process of steaming groats and pressing them between rollers to form flakes.

Rolling pin A thick, heavy, smooth cylindrical rod of hardwood with handles on each end designed for efficient rolling out of raw doughs.

Rounding Molding a kneaded yeast dough into a round shape by forming a tight outer skin.

Rye meal Coarse meal ground from the whole rye berry.

Scaling The professional term for measuring ingredients or cutting the dough into portions before shaping.

Sheave Professional term for shoving the breads off the peel into the hearth oven.

Slurry The first stage of activating the yeast in water with a pinch of sugar. Also referred to as the yeast suspension.

Soft wheat Produces flour low in protein (6 to 10 percent) used especially for cakes and biscuits.

Sour cream Cream that is curdled with lactic-acid producing bacteria to produce a thick and smooth tangy cream.

Spatula Flexible flat blade attached to a handle used to scrape mixtures from the sides of a bowl or to move baked goods.

Spiral The spiral is a popular shape for forming yeast doughs and rolls, as it retains its shape perfectly after baking. Spiral-shape breads are called *Schnecken* (snails) in German-speaking countries.

Sponge A bread starter combining some liquid with yeast and flour to form a thick mixture that ferments as it stands before the initial mixing of the dough.

Stone ground A term to describe flours milled by a slow grinding process which does not generate the heat that destroys delicate vitamins in ground grains; the method retains the natural sweet flavor of the grain.

Straight flour Professional term for the generic grade of white flour sold in supermarkets.

Streusel From a German word meaning litter or dust, streusel is a rubbed mixture of flour, sugar, and cold butter used as a topping or filling in sweet breads.

Summer wheat Grain that is sown in the spring and harvested in the fall.

Tempered Professional term for the separation process when wheat is soaked in water to soften the bran layer and soften the endosperm before milling.

Texture The inside grain or crumb.

Torta An Italian sweet or savory tart or pie; also a cake.

Turnover A rustic half-moon, triangular, or rectangluar pastry case folded over a sweet or savory filling. It may be shaped into full- or individual-size pie.

Tutové The traditional heavy, ribbed French rolling pin designed for rolling in and distributing the butter between dough layers in croissants and Danish pastries.

Unbleached flour Naturally aged wheat flour. If slightly aged with potassium bromate, unbleached flour is labeled bromated.

Unsaturated oils Corn, sunflower, olive, canola, walnut, almond, and other pure cold-pressed oils are the best for breads, each adding its own unique flavor. They are used as an alternative to butter, margarine, and coconut and palm oils, which all have a high fatty acid composition and are highly saturated.

Viennoiserie Collection of milk breads and sophisticated yeast techniques used today in France, including the croissant and brioche, brought to the royal kitchens during the eighteenth century by court bakers from Vienna.

Volume The size the dough reaches when rising or when baked.

Well method Flour is formed into a mound with a depression in the center for mixing. In the authentic method, the mixing is done directly on the bench without a bowl.

Wheat A cultivated grass plant. The grain, which is ground for flour, is made up of three parts—the endosperm, the germ, and the aleurone, or husk.

Whole grain A groat or berry that retains both its germ and bran coating or a product containing those when ground.

Whole wheat flour Flour made by grinding the entire kernel of hard wheat to different degrees of fineness.

Whole wheat pastry flour Ground from soft wheat.

Winter wheat Grain that is sown in the fall—primarily laying dormant over the winter—and harvested in the summer.

Yeast (*Saccharomyces cerevisiae*) A one-celled plant with no cholorophyll that feeds on complex carbohydrates and sugar to reproduce rapidly and raise bread and ferment beer.

Yield The number of loaves that a recipe will make.

Zest The colored outer portion of the skin of citrus fruits.

Index